BROADMAN COMMENTS

December 1998 - February 1999

BROADMAN COMMENTS

December 1998 - February 1999

13 User-Friendly Bible Study Lessons

ROBERT J. DEAN

WILLIAM E. ANDERSON

JAMES E. TAULMAN

BROADMAN
&HOLMAN
PUBLISHERS

Nashville, Tennessee

This material was published first in *Broadman Comments, 1998–1999*

ISBN: 0–8054–1759–1

The Outlines of the International Sunday School Lessons, Uniform Series, are
copyrighted by the Committee on the Uniform Series and are used by permission.

Dewey Decimal Classification: 268.61
Subject Heading: SUNDAY SCHOOL LESSONS—COMMENTARIES

Broadman Comments *is published quarterly by Broadman & Holman Publishers,
127 Ninth Avenue, North, Nashville, Tennessee 37234*

*When ordered with other church literature, it sells for $5.99 per quarter.
Second class postage paid at Nashville, Tennessee*

ISSN: 0068–2721

POSTMASTER: Send address change to *Broadman Comments,*
Customer Service Center, 127 Ninth Avenue, North
Nashville, Tennessee 37234

Library of Congress Catalog Card Number: 45–437
Printed in the United States of America

WRITERS

STUDYING THE BIBLE

Robert J. Dean continues the theological traditions of *Broadman Comments* while adding his own fresh insights. Dean is retired from the Baptist Sunday School Board and is a Th.D. graduate of New Orleans Seminary.

APPLYING THE BIBLE

William E. Anderson has been pastor of Calvary Baptist Church, Clearwater, Florida, since 1975. Calvary's weekly services are telecast on various local stations and by satellite over Christian Network, Inc., on the Dish Network.

TEACHING THE BIBLE

James E. Taulman is a freelance writer in Nashville, Tennessee. Prior to that, Taulman was an editor of adult Sunday school materials for the Baptist Sunday School Board.

Scripture passages are from the authorized King James Version of the Bible.

Contents

GOD CALLS ANEW IN JESUS CHRIST

Contents

God Calls Anew in Jesus Christ

INTRODUCTION

This quarter is a survey of the New Testament. There are several ways to survey the New Testament: select high points in chronological order, sample different kinds of New Testament books, or look at important themes. This quarter's survey combines these approaches.

Unit I, "The Good News of Jesus Christ," highlights in four lessons who Jesus is, how the good news was first preached and then written, the birth of Jesus (Christmas), and His resurrection and continuing presence.

Unit II, "Good News for Daily Living," presents four important teachings of Jesus in the Gospels: love, greed, true greatness, and forgiveness.

Unit III, "Good News for Changing Times," presents five issues faced by the early Christians: taking the good news to all people, living as citizens of heaven in an earthly kingdom, maintaining unity of spirit and avoiding disruptive dissension, fulfilling a ministry of reconciliation, and living in confident hope.

P A G E

Cycle of 1998–2004

1998–1999	1999–2000	2000–2001	2001–2002	2002–2003	2003–2004
Old Testament Survey	Exodus Leviticus Numbers Deuteronomy Joshua	Judges 1, 2 Samuel 1 Chronicles 1 Kings 1–11 2 Chronicles 1–9	Parables Miracles Sermon on the Mount	2 Kings 18–25 2 Chronicles 29–36 Jeremiah Lamentations Ezekiel Habakkuk Zephaniah	James 1, 2 Peter 1, 2, 3 John Jude
New Testament Survey	Matthew	Luke	Isaiah 9; 11; 40–66; Ruth Jonah Nahum	Personalities of the NT	Christmas Esther Job Ecclesiastes Song of Solomon
John	1, 2 Corinthians	Acts	Romans Galatians	Mark	The Cross 1, 2 Thessalonians Revelation
Genesis	Ephesians Philippians Colossians Philemon	1 Kings 12– 2 Kings 17 2 Chronicles 10–28 Isaiah 1–39 Amos Hosea Micah	Psalms Proverbs	Ezra Nehemiah Daniel Joel Obadiah Haggai Zechariah Malachi	Hebrews 1, 2 Timothy Titus

Who Is This?

Background Passages: Hebrews 1:1–4; Matthew 16:13–26
Focal Passages: Hebrews 1:1–4; Matthew 16:13–23

Jesus Christ is the heart of the Bible. The Old Testament points forward to Him. The Gospels tell of His coming, life, death, and resurrection. The rest of the New Testament tells how His gospel was spread and how Christians were taught to live in the way of Christ. Two key passages in this lesson focus on the identity of Jesus. Hebrews 1:1–4 exalts Him as God's supreme revelation in His Son. Matthew 16:13–23 focuses on a crucial point in the Gospels—when Jesus began to teach His disciples that He was the Suffering Servant, who would suffer, die, and be raised from the dead.

▶**Study Aim:** *To testify to who Jesus is.*

STUDYING THE BIBLE

OUTLINE AND SUMMARY
  I. **God's Supreme Revelation (Heb. 1:1–4)**
      1. **God has spoken (1:1–2a)**
      2. **Sevenfold exaltation of Christ (1:2b–3)**
      3. **Superior to the angels (1:4)**
  II. **The Crucified Messiah (Matt. 16:13–26)**
      1. **Peter's confession (16:13–16)**
      2. **Christ's church (16:17–19)**
      3. **Christ must suffer, die, and be raised (Matt. 16:20–21)**
      4. **The cross—stumbling block (16:22–23)**
      5. **A cross for Jesus' followers (16:24–26)**

God revealed Himself partially in Old Testament times, but His fullest revelation was in His Son (Heb. 1:1–2a). The Son is the eternal Son who died for our sins and was exalted by God (Heb. 1:2b–3). He is superior to the angels and all aspects of the old covenant revelation (Heb. 1:4). He is the Messiah, the Son of the living God (Matt. 16:13–16). Christ builds His church so that death cannot overcome it (Matt. 16:17–19). The Messiah must suffer, die, and be raised from the dead (Matt. 16:20–21). When Peter rebuked Jesus for saying this, Jesus accused him of becoming an instrument of Satan (Matt. 16:22–23). Not only must Jesus die, but also His followers must walk the way of the cross (Matt. 16:24–26).

I. God's Supreme Revelation (Heb. 1:1–4)

1. God has spoken (1:1–2a)

   1 God, who at sundry times and in divers manners spake in time past unto the fathers by the prophets,
   2 Hath in these last days spoken unto us by his Son.

Skeptics claim that God—if there be a God—has been silent in a world of suffering and injustices. The Bible denies this charge by insisting that God has spoken. Verse 1 describes how God spoke in Old Testament times, and verse 2 points to how God has spoken His final word in His Son.

Verse 1 is a concise statement of God's revelation in the Old Testament. "The fathers" are the generations to whom God spoke "in time past." "The prophets" referred to all those through whom God spoke during the age of promise, whether they were called prophets, kings, priests, or wise men. "At sundry times and in divers manners" refers to the variety of ways in which God spoke.

Verse 2a uses three contrasts to highlight the fulfillment of the earlier revelation:

1. "In time past" contrasts with "in these last days." Jesus Christ divided history. From the New Testament perspective, His incarnate ministry marked the final stage of God's redemptive plan. In one sense, the entire New Testament era is "the last days" (see 2 Cor. 6:2; 1 John 2:18).
2. "The fathers" is contrasted with "us." This contrasts the recipients of the two stages of divine revelation. The people of Old Testament times heard a partial revelation, but we are privileged to stand in the full noontime of the age of fulfillment.
3. "The prophets" are contrasted with "his Son." The prophets were human beings through whom God spoke His messages, but the Son is the eternal Word made flesh in whom God revealed Himself. The word "Son"—as used for Jesus—does not imply a being that had a point of beginning. Hebrews 1:2b–3 and many other New Testament passages emphasize that Christ is the eternal Son of God who became truly human and remained fully divine in order to reveal God and to save sinners (John 1:1–18; Phil. 2:6–11).

Remember how the Hebrews thought of the word *son.* "A son was to be like his father. He was not only to look like his father but also to reflect his father's ideas and often to follow his father's occupation. In other words, if a Jew had met a man's son, he felt that he also knew the father. Therefore, Jesus said, "He that hath seen me hath seen the Father" (John 14:9). If we want to know what God is like, we read what the four Gospels tell us about what Jesus said and did.

2. Sevenfold exaltation of Christ (1:2b–3)

2 Whom he hath appointed heir of all things, by whom also he made the worlds;

3 Who being the brightness of his glory, and the express image of his person, and upholding all things by the word of his power, when he had by himself purged our sins, sat down on the right hand of the Majesty on high.

This sevenfold exaltation has the feel of a hymn of praise.

1. The eternal Son of God is the heir of all things—people and the created universe.
2. God created the worlds through the divine Son (John 1:1–3).

3. The Son reveals the full splendor of the divine presence (glory; John 1:14).
4. Jesus Christ is "the express image" or exact likeness of God.
5. Jesus upholds and moves God's redemptive purpose toward its consummation.
6. Jesus, through His sacrificial death, provided a way for sins to be cleansed.
7. Jesus, following His victorious resurrection, was exalted to the place of honor at God's right hand.

3. Superior to the angels (1:4)

4 Being made so much better than the angels, as he hath by inheritance obtained a more excellent name than they.

Angels were considered to be mediators of the old covenant. The content of the book of Hebrews shows how the new covenant revelation of God in His Son is superior to all aspects of the old covenant revelation: prophets, angels, Moses, Levitical priests, animal sacrifices. His superiority to the angels is presented in Hebrews 1:4–14.

II. The Crucified Messiah (Matt. 16:13–26)

1. Peter's confession (16:13–16)

13 When Jesus came into the coasts of Caesarea Philippi, he asked his disciples, saying, Whom do men say that I the Son of man am?

14 And they said, Some say that thou art John the Baptist: some, Elias; and others, Jeremias, or one of the prophets.

15 He saith unto them, But whom say ye that I am?

16 And Simon Peter answered and said, Thou art the Christ, the Son of the living God.

Most of Jesus' ministry had been in Galilee; now He led His disciples to Caesarea Philippi, about twenty-five miles north of the Sea of Galilee. There he asked the disciples who people thought He was. John the Baptist had been put to death by Herod Antipas, but Herod had a superstitious fear that Jesus was John raised from the dead (Matt. 14:2). Others shared Herod's view. Most others thought Jesus was Elijah (Elias), Jeremiah (Jeremias), or one of the other prophets. Thus, the people saw Jesus as no more than another prophet or perhaps as the forerunner of the Messiah.

When Jesus asked the disciples about their own views, Simon confessed faith in Jesus as the Christ. *Christ* is the Greek word for Messiah. The words *Messiah* and *Christ* mean "anointed one" and refer to the promised King of David's line (2 Sam. 7:12–16). After the kingdom of Judah fell, this hope of a coming king had sustained the Jews for several centuries. Many Jews expected the Messiah to be a military, political king. Simon also professed faith in Jesus as the divine Son of God, which the disciples had already recognized (see Matt. 14:33).

2. Christ's church (16:17–19)

17 And Jesus answered and said unto him, Blessed art thou, Simon Bar-jona: for flesh and blood hath not revealed it unto thee, but my Father which is in heaven.

18 And I say also unto thee, That thou art Peter, and upon this rock I will build my church; and the gates of hell shall not prevail against it.

19 And I will give unto thee the keys of the kingdom of heaven; and whatsoever thou shalt bind on earth shall be bound in heaven: and whatsoever thou shalt loose on earth shall be loosed in heaven.

These have been among the most controversial verses throughout Christian history. On one hand, these verses have been used to justify Peter as the first pope and one church as having the power to forgive sins. On the other hand, many have strongly denied that Jesus intended to establish an ecclesiastical authority residing in Peter and his supposed successors.

The crux of the debate centers around the meaning of "rock." The name *Peter* means "rock." Therefore, some see Peter as the foundation of the church. However, even if he was, he was acting as a representative of the apostles, whose testimony to Christ formed the foundation of the church (Eph. 2:20). No one is the ultimate foundation of the church other than Christ Himself (1 Cor. 3:11).

The keys of the kingdom were given to all the apostles in Matthew 18:18–19. The keys refer to the responsibility of the apostles and later witnesses for Christ. We can open the door to the kingdom by sharing the gospel.

The real emphasis in verses 17–19 ought to be on the church that Christ was going to build. Jesus was referring to the redeemed people of God, whether on earth or in heaven.

The word translated "hell" in verse 18 is the Greek word *hades*, not *gehenna*. The former word refers sometimes to a place of punishment (Luke 16:23), but its basic meaning is death and the grave. The latter word refers to the place of punishment. Jesus promised that the power of death would not be able to hold God's people prisoners (Rev. 1:18).

3. Christ must suffer, die, and be raised (16:20–21)

20 Then charged he his disciples that they should tell no man that he was Jesus the Christ.

21 From that time forth began Jesus to shew unto his disciples how that he must go unto Jerusalem, and suffer many things of the elders and the chief priests and scribes, and be killed, and be raised again the third day.

No doubt the disciples were puzzled by Jesus' command not to tell anyone that He was the Messiah. Christians today may also be puzzled in light of the Lord's later emphasis on telling the world (Matt. 28:18–20). Jesus knew that most Jews were looking for a military, political Messiah. He feared that people would assume that He was the kind of Messiah that they were expecting (John 6:15). Verse 22 shows that this was Peter's view of the Messiah.

Jesus was indeed the Messiah, but He had come to conquer sin and death, not Rome and economic problems. He knew that He could save people from sin and death only by fulfilling Isaiah's prophecy of the Suffering Servant (Isa. 53). Therefore, He tried to build on Peter's confession by introducing the disciples to the necessity of His suffering, death, and resurrection.

4. The cross—a stumbling block (16:22–23)

22 Then Peter took him, and began to rebuke him, saying, Be it far from thee, Lord: this shall not be unto thee.

23 But he turned, and said unto Peter, Get thee behind me, Satan: thou art an offence unto me: for thou savourest not the things that be of God, but those that be of men.

Peter, who only a moment before had been commended for responding to the revelation of Jesus as Christ, now presumed to rebuke Jesus for saying that He must suffer and die. This idea was totally alien to anything Peter had believed about what the Messiah would do.

Jesus, in turn, strongly rebuked the disciple whom he had just commended. Jesus used strong words to accuse Peter of being an instrument of Satan to once again tempt Jesus to find some easier way of fulfilling His mission than dying on the cross.

5. A cross for Jesus' followers (16:24–26)

Jesus quickly followed up by telling them that not only must He go to the cross but also that they too must deny themselves, take up their crosses, and follow Him (16:24). Only by giving one's life would a person find his life; while those who tried to look out only for themselves would lose everything (16:25). To exchange one's soul for anything is not a good bargain (16:26).

SUMMARY OF BIBLE TRUTHS

1. God revealed Himself in various ways in Old Testament times.
2. God's fullest revelation is in His Son Jesus Christ.
3. Jesus builds His church so that death cannot overcome it.
4. Jesus is the Messiah and Son of God, who overcame sin and death through His death and resurrection.

APPLYING THE BIBLE

1. How to get the world right. Our focus today is on the person of Christ. Some young parents gave their son a picture-puzzle for Christmas one year. On one side of the puzzle was a picture of the earth, and on the other, a picture of an artist's rendering of the face of Christ. They heard the boy telling his younger sister, "It's easy! If you get Jesus' face right, the whole world will be right, too." That's what the Christian church has been saying for almost two thousand years. And that's what millions have discovered to be true through those two thousand years.

2. God has revealed Himself to us in Christ. I am not sure one can prioritize miracles, but it has been my theory for many years that the greatest of all things God has done, having created the universe, was to reveal Himself to us. Everything hinges on that! Today's lesson reminds us that God's revelation centers in Christ. Jesus has shown us the Father. John 1:14 teaches us that God became flesh and dwelt (or "tabernacled") among us. John 1:18 tells us that Jesus "declared" the Father to us. The word *declared* translates the Greek word *eksago,* from which we get our word *exegesis.* If the pastor preaches an "exegetical" message, he pulls out of the text what is actually there. Jesus did not just preach an exegetical message about the Father: Jesus *was* an exegetical message about the Father personified! Without Jesus we would know nothing about the Father except a few general truths given in the natural world (see Rom. 1:18f). That is why Jesus must always be the center of all theological study—to the professional and the layperson.

3. Many names for Jesus. I have a book in which the author lists and explains the meaning of 365 names of Christ in the Bible.[1] Why so many names for Jesus? Because Jesus' names signify His character and because Jesus' personality is of such an oceanic magnitude that many names are required to portray Him accurately.

4. The unfathomable Christ. In Ephesians 3:8, Paul tells us that he preached "among the gentiles the unsearchable riches of Christ." The Greek word translated "unsearchable" (*aneksichniaston*) is used twice in the New Testament (here and in Rom. 11:33). This word means "incapable of being searched out" or "untraceable." Ancient Greek sailors also used this word to mean "unfathomable" or "too deep to measure." Think of it! Paul is confessing that he could never exhaust his theme! Could never tell it all! Could never touch bottom! What an encouragement to all who teach or preach about Jesus!

5. Christ came down. Perhaps the finest of the many millions of poetic references to Christ is that from John Milton's "On the Morning of Christ's Nativity":

> That glorious form, that light unsufferable,
> And that far-beaming blaze of majesty,
> He laid aside; and here with us to be,
> Forsook the courts of everlasting day,
> And chose with us a darksome house of mortal clay.

6. Jesus in first place. Guess who has the most reference entries in the Library of Congress? The first three are Jesus Christ, William Shakespeare, and Abraham Lincoln! We might debate about who should be in second and third place, but there is no question about who should be in first place. Just think about Jesus' influence on western civilization, and therefore, of course, on America!

7. Jesus was a prophet. Look carefully again at today's text and list the various prophecies—predictions of future events—Jesus gave. What others do you recollect that He gave? How many of Jesus' prophecies have not yet come true? These will certainly come true in the future. List five implications of this fact. We can begin with number 1: "We can know for sure and for certain that if we are His, we will spend eternity with Him in heaven." Now continue your list!

8. The heart of the story. I have a collection of over two hundred books about Abraham Lincoln. I have noticed that every author emphasizes different characteristics of Lincoln. In fact, it is sometimes very difficult to get at the full truth (as, for instance, Lincoln's precise relationship with Ann Rutledge). Every biographer chooses what to include and what to leave out. But the Holy Spirit does precisely the same thing with Jesus! He didn't have room—or didn't take it—to tell everything about Jesus. John said that if everything Jesus did were written down, "the world itself could not contain the books that should be written!" (John 21:25) If you were to list seven facts about Jesus that would best identify Him to somebody who knew nothing about Him, what would those seven facts be? How are our lives affected by those seven facts?

TEACHING THE BIBLE

▶ *Main Idea:* Jesus is God's supreme revelation and our only Savior.
▶ *Suggested Teaching Aim:* To help adults to testify that Jesus is God's supreme revelation and our only Savior.

A TEACHING OUTLINE

1. *God's Supreme Revelation (Heb. 1:1–4)*
2. *The Crucified Messiah (Matt. 16:13–26)*

Introduce the Bible Study

Summarize the unit Introduction to introduce the Bible study. Make a unit poster with the three unit headings and the thirteen lesson titles and dates on it. Use this each week to indicate the lesson so members can see the progression of the quarter's study.

Search for Biblical Truth

On a chalkboard or a large sheet of paper, write this chart without the italicized phrases (you will add them later):

Revelation Contrasted

	Earlier	**Later**
When?	*In times past*	*In these last days*
To Whom?	*The fathers*	*Us*
By Whom?	*The prophets*	*The Son*

Ask members to open their Bibles to Hebrews 1:1–2a. Ask: When did God make His earlier revelation? (In times past.) His later revelation? (In these last days.) To whom did God make His earlier revelation? (The fathers.) His later revelation? (Us.) By whom did God make his earlier revelation? (The prophets.) His later revelation? (The Son.) What was the purpose of both revelations? (To reveal God.) Which revelation was most successful in doing this? Read this statement: "If we want to know what God is like, we read what the four Gospels tell us about what Jesus said and did."

Ask members to look at Hebrews 1:2b–3. **IN ADVANCE**, copy the seven statements of exaltation on small pieces of paper and give them to seven members to read aloud. Form groups of three or four people each, distribute paper and pencils, and ask members to write a hymn of praise to Jesus using these verses.

On a chalkboard write: *Jesus is greater than:* Ask members to look at Hebrews 1:4 and identify who Jesus is greater than and list these under the heading. (1. angels.) Ask members to look at these passages in Hebrews and identify others to whom Jesus is superior: 1:1 (2. prophets); 3:3; (3. Moses); 5:5 (4. priests); 9:25–28 (5. sacrifices).

Ask members to turn to Matthew 16:13–16 and find three others to whom Jesus is superior. (6. John, 7. Elijah, and 8. Jeremiah.) Now write *Jesus is:* at the bottom of the list. Ask, According to Matthew 16:16, who is Jesus? (1. The Christ, 2. The Son of the living God.)

Now add *Jesus gives:* to the list. Ask members to look at Matthew 16:17–21 and find two things Jesus gives to us. (1. His church, 2. keys.)

Prepare a brief lecture using the material in "Studying the Bible" to explain what Jesus meant by "church," "rock," "keys," "hell" and why Jesus did not want the disciples to tell others He was the Messiah.

Ask members to read silently Matthew 16:22–23. Ask, Have you done anything this week that would make Jesus speak to you like this?

Give the Truth a Personal Focus

Briefly review the list. Ask, If Jesus is superior to all of these, what keeps us from following Him? Be sensitive to the leadership of the Holy Spirit, but if you have people in your class who have not accepted Christ as God's supreme revelation and their only Savior, urge them to do so. Close in prayer that all may have a renewed understanding of the superiority of Jesus.

---

1. Herbert C. Gabhart, *The Name Above Every Name* (Nashville: Broadman, 1986).

Good News: Spoken and Written

Background Passages: Luke 1:1–4; 1 Corinthians 15:1–4;
1 John 1:1–4
Focal Passages: Luke 1:1–4; 1 Corinthians 15:1–4;
1 John 1:1–4

The Greek word translated "gospel" means "good news." Luke 1:1–4 introduces one of the four books we call "Gospels." First Corinthians 15:1–4 describes the heart of the good news the early Christians preached. First John 1:1–4 is the testimony of an eyewitness to the events of Jesus' incarnate ministry.

▶**Study Aim:** To describe how the good news was spoken and written.

STUDYING THE BIBLE

OUTLINE AND SUMMARY

   I. **Writing the Good News (Luke 1:1–4)**
      1. **Writing the testimony of eyewitnesses (1:1–2)**
      2. **Luke and his Gospel (1:3–4)**
  II. **Good News of Salvation (1 Cor. 15:1–4)**
      1. **Good news preached and believed (15:1–2)**
      2. **Heart of the good news (15:3–4)**
 III. **Testimony of an Eyewitness (1 John 1:1–4)**
      1. **Eyewitnesses of the Word of life (1:1–2)**
      2. **Purposes of the testimony of eyewitnesses (1:3–4)**

Luke was one of those who wrote the testimony of people who had been with Jesus (Luke 1:1–2). After careful investigation, Luke wrote a Gospel expressing the certainty of the good news (Luke 1:3–4). Paul preached the good news that brought salvation to those who believed (1 Cor. 15:1–2). The good news was that Christ died for our sins and was raised from the dead (15:3–4). As an eyewitness, John testified to the reality of the deity and humanity of Jesus (1 John 1:1–2). He wrote so that his readers might have fellowship with the Lord and know His joy (1 John 1:3–4).

I. Writing the Good News (1:1–4)

1. Writing the testimony of eyewitnesses (1:1–2)

    1 Forasmuch as many have taken in hand to set forth in order a declaration of those things which are most surely believed among us,

    2 Even as they delivered them unto us, which from the beginning were eyewitnesses, and ministers of the word.

Luke 1:1–4 gives insight into how the good news was first spoken and then written. Verse 1 shows that Luke was not the first person to put the story of Jesus into written form.

Verse 2 shows that Luke was not an eyewitness to the events of Jesus' life, death, and resurrection. In fact, Paul's letters reveal that Luke was a gentile convert and a physician (Col. 4:11–14; 2 Tim. 4:11). The Gospel he wrote shows that he was also a careful historian as well as a committed and informed believer.

Luke used the word *delivered* to describe how the apostles faithfully transmitted the events of the good news. Although Luke himself was not an eyewitness, he based what he wrote on the testimony of eyewitnesses—whether in spoken or written form. The apostles told and retold what Jesus had said and done. Others heard, learned, and passed on these events. For a long time, this was done only in spoken form; but eventually, the good news began to be put into written form.

Four factors ensure the accuracy of what eventually was written:
1. People of that day were much more skilled at remembering and retelling what they had heard.
2. The apostles were around to ensure the accuracy of the spoken message.
3. The New Testament books were written either by eyewitnesses or on the basis of the testimony of eyewitnesses.
4. The Holy Spirit guided in all this.

Three facts also explain why they began to put the Gospels into written form:
1. As the apostles began to die, a written record was needed for the future.
2. Many letters had been written and were being circulated among the churches.
3. The Greeks and Romans relied more on written communication than did the Jews.

2. Luke and his Gospel (1:3–4)

> **3 It seemed good to me also, having had perfect understanding of all things from the very first, to write unto thee in order, most excellent Theophilus,**
>
> **4 That thou mightest know the certainty of those things, wherein thou hast been instructed.**

Verses 3–4 reveal three facts about Luke and his Gospel:

1. Before writing, Luke made a careful study of the coming, ministry, teachings, death, and resurrection of Jesus. "Perfect" means "careful." "Understanding" means "investigation." "From the very first" refers to the beginning of Jesus' life, not to Luke's discipleship. Luke was not an eyewitness, but he made a careful study about all that eyewitnesses said and wrote about Jesus from the very beginning of His life.

2. Luke wrote a complete and orderly account of the events of the gospel. The mention of the "very first" implied that Luke intended to go back to the beginning. Thus His Gospel begins with the announcements of the births of John the Baptist and Jesus (Luke 1:4–35). Of course, none of the Gospels records everything Jesus said and did (John 21:25). "In order" means that Luke followed an overall chronological sequence.

3. Luke wrote as a believer to affirm the certainty of the Christian good news. Luke was a careful writer and historian of the story of Jesus; but he was, first of all, a convinced believer. The Gospel of Luke and the Book of Acts were both addressed to Theophilus (Luke 1:3; Acts 1:1). He may have been a convert or perhaps a seeker; however, he had been instructed in the Christian good news. Luke wrote to assure Theophilus of its certainty.

II. Good News of Salvation (1 Cor. 15:1–4)

1. Good news preached and believed (15:1–2)

> **1 Moreover, brethren, I declare unto you the gospel which I preached unto you, which also ye have received, and wherein ye stand;**
>
> **2 By which also ye are saved, if ye keep in memory what I preached unto you, unless ye have believed in vain.**

Most of the New Testament Letters were written before the Gospels were written. First Corinthians 15:1–4 shows that Paul preached the good news in Corinth (Acts 18:1–18). Shortly after that he wrote a letter reminding them of the gospel he had preached (1 Cor. 16:9). Paul also reminded them that they had received the good news, had been saved, and were now standing in this gospel.

The last part of verse 2 reflects a problem mentioned in 1 Corinthians 15:12. The Corinthians apparently did not question the resurrection of Jesus Christ; however, some had doubts about the future resurrection of believers. Most Greeks did not believe in any life after death, but some believed in immortality of the soul. However, Greek philosophers scoffed at the idea of resurrection of the body. Chapter 15 emphasizes that faith in the resurrection of Christ is inseparable from the hope of future resurrection.

Note

2. Heart of the good news (15:3–4)

> **3 For I delivered unto you first of all that which I also received, how that Christ died for our sins according to the scriptures;**
>
> **4 And that he was buried, and that he rose again the third day according to the scriptures.**

Like Luke, Paul had "delivered" the good news to which the apostles bore witness. Of course, Paul considered himself an apostle to whom the risen Lord made a special appearance (1 Cor. 15:8–10). Verses 3–4 summarize the heart of the good news of salvation preached by the apostles: the atoning death of Jesus Christ, His burial, and His resurrection from the dead—according to the Scriptures.

"Christ died for our sins." In last week's lesson, we saw how Peter and others failed to understand Jesus' prediction of His death and resurrection. Only after His resurrection were they enabled to see His crucifixion as a victory. The risen Lord opened the Scriptures to them and showed them how this was taught in the Word of God (Luke 24:44–46).

They came to see that God's purpose in the Crucifixion was to provide atonement for human sin.

"He was buried." Why did Paul list the burial as part of the good news? Remember the problem mentioned in 1 Corinthians 15:12. The burial of Jesus showed the reality of His death and thus set the stage for the reality of His bodily resurrection.

"He rose again." This event also was according to the Scriptures (Acts 2:24–36). The cross and the resurrection are inseparable. The cross without the resurrection would have been a defeat. The resurrection would have failed to atone for human sins. Together they constitute God's good news of salvation from sin and death.

III. Testimony of an Eyewitness (1 John 1:1–4)
1. Eyewitnesses of the Word of life (1 John 1:1–2)

1 That which was from the beginning, which we have heard, which we have seen with our eyes, which we have looked upon, and our hands have handled, of the Word of life;

2 (For the life was manifested, and we have seen it, and bear witness, and shew unto you that eternal life, which was with the Father, and was manifested unto us).

John has the distinction of being the only person to write so many different kinds of books in the New Testament. Paul wrote the most in number, but all of his were letters. John wrote a Gospel, three letters, and the book of Revelation. Most New Testament students notice parallels between the prologues to the Gospel of John (1:1–18) and to 1 John (1:1–4). Here are some of these:

"The beginning" (1 John 1:1; John 1:1)

"Word" (1 John 1:1; John 1:1, 14)

"With the Father" (1 John 1:2); "with God" (John 1:1–2)

"Life" (1 John 1:1–2; John 1:4)

"Looked upon" (1 John 1:1); same word as "beheld" (John 1:14)

"We" (1 John 1:1–4; John 1:14)

Both prologues emphasize two things: (1) The eternal Word who was with the Father and (2) the reality of His Incarnation. Both passages are designed to counteract a false teaching that was just beginning to have its evil effect. The Gnostics taught that Jesus was truly divine but only appeared to be human.

Notice how John emphasized the experience of the eyewitnesses as a basis for affirming the reality of the Word made flesh. John used "we" for himself and the other apostles, who experienced not only the divine power of Jesus but also the reality of His full humanity. John used these words that described various senses: "Have heard," "have seen with our eyes," "have looked upon," and "our hands have handled." John left no doubt that the Jesus they knew was fully divine and fully human.

2. Purposes of the testimony of eyewitnesses (1:3–4)

3 That which we have seen and heard declare we unto you, that ye also may have fellowship with us: and truly our fellowship is with the Father, and with his Son Jesus Christ.

4 And these things write we unto you, that your joy may be full.

Three words define the purposes of the testimony of the eyewitnesses:

1. Life. Both 1 John and John's Gospel make frequent use of "life" and "eternal life" (John 1:4; 3:16). Obviously, Jesus came to bring "life" that is abundant (John 10:10) and eternal. This life begins when a person believes and passes from spiritual death to life in Christ (John 3:16; 5:24).

2. Fellowship. This word translates a Greek word meaning "having something in common." Thus, it has the idea of sharing with, communion with, and being in union with. John used the word only four times—all in 1 John 1:3–7. Believers have fellowship with the apostles in this sense: Believers—like the apostles—are one "with the Father, and with His Son Jesus Christ" (1 John 1:3). Because "we have fellowship with him" (1 John 1:6), "we have fellowship one with another" (1 John 1:7).

3. Joy. Many people consider Christ and Christians to be kill joys; yet Jesus saw Himself as a joy-giver (John 15:11). The apostles saw themselves as joy-givers (1 John 1:1; 2 Cor. 1:24; Phil. 4:4). Christian joy is dependent only on a right relation with God and with others, not on outward circumstances (Matt. 5:10–12; Rom. 5:1–4; James 1:2–4; 1 Pet. 1:6–7).

SUMMARY OF BIBLE TRUTHS

1. The good news of Jesus Christ is the best news the world has ever heard.
2. The heart of the good news is the atoning death and victorious resurrection of Jesus Christ.
3. Eyewitnesses first preached the good news and ensured its truth.
4. The New Testament is the inspired testimony of the eyewitnesses in permanent written form.

APPLYING THE BIBLE

1. Jesus—the Lamb of God. According to the Bible, Jesus was
- a spotless lamb,
- a subordinate lamb,
- a shorn lamb,
- a silent lamb,
- a suffering lamb,
- a substitionary lamb, and
- a saving lamb.

2. The glorious gospel. Everybody loves good news. And the gospel is good news! Dr. Baldwin had pastored one church for over forty-one years. He said, "At thirty, after examining the philosophies and religions of the world, I said that nothing is better than the gospel of Christ. At forty, when burdens pressed heavily and the years seemed to haste, I said that nothing is better than the gospel. At fifty, when there were empty chairs at home and the grave-diggers had done their job, I said, nothing is to be compared to the gospel. At <u>sixty</u>, when my second sight saw through the illusions and vanities of earthly things, I said there is nothing but the gospel. And then, at seventy, amid many limitations and privations, I sang:

> Should all the forms which men devise,
> Attack my faith with treacherous art,
> I'd call them vanity and lies,
> And bind the gospel to my heart."[1]

3. Jesus died in my place. Jesus died a vicarious death, for He died in our place. H. C. Thiessen writes, "Vicarious suffering is suffering endured by one person in the stead of another, that is, in his place. It necessarily supposes the exemption of the party in whose place the suffering is endured. A 'vicar' is a substitute, one who takes the place of another, and acts in his stead."[2]

4. Who stole Christmas? Charles Colson presents this information from a "re-imaging" conference on theology: "Aruna Gnanadason, of the World Council of Churches, said 'her' god has nothing to do with the crucifixion. The 'cruel and violent death of Christ on the cross, sanction(s) violence against the powerless in society,' she charged. Delores Williams of Union Theological Seminary chimed in: 'I don't think we need folks hanging on crosses and blood dripping and wierd stuff . . . we don't need atonement, we just need to listen to the god within.'"[3]

5. A Christless church? The late George Cornell of the Associated Press reported on a religious meeting in 1959 entitled "Church Delegates Cut Special Ties to Jesus." According to Cornell, about "1,000 representatives of . . . two free-minded churches (giving) strong backing Thursday night to a merger, with preliminary balloting rejecting any special ties to Jesus." He went on to say that "A joint assembly of the delegates of the two churches voted to eliminate special emphasis on Jesus as the crux of their proposed union." The vote was finalized, and the two churches merged, having taken an anti-Jesus stand, which they <u>still</u> maintain. Contrast that with what John Donne once said about Jesus: "All knowledge that begins not, and ends not with His glory, is but a giddy, but a vertiginous circle, but an elaborate and exquisite ignorance." I vote with Donne! And the entire church has for almost 2,000 years!

6. We know Jesus personally. The apostolic witnesses had experienced a personal encounter with Jesus, so they could speak from first hand knowledge about Him. I was once asked to introduce a speaker to a large group of community leaders, but I had never met the speaker personally! Take it from me: That is a hard assignment! Luke wrote this of the people in Jerusalem: "Now when they saw the boldness of Peter and John, and perceived that they were unlearned and ignorant men, they marvelled; and they took knowledge of them, that they had been with Jesus" (Acts 4:13). The apostles themselves said, "For we cannot but speak the things which we have seen and heard" (Acts 4:20). And remember what the Jewish "vagabond" exorcists experienced when they

re-read

tried to use Jesus' name to cast out demons—when they had never met Jesus personally! (Acts 19:13–16).

__7. The power of Christian witness.__ Historian Robert A. Baker lists four reasons why the witness of the early Christians was so powerful:
1. Paganism could not satisfy hungry hearts.
2. The welter of religions of every description clamoring for devotees could not compete with God's revelation in Christ.
3. Christians became missionaries; the sacred fire leaped from friend to friend.
4. Christians had a burning conviction that Christ alone could save the lost world about them. They believed that there was no time to be lost since the return of Christ was imminent.[5]

TEACHING THE BIBLE

Good News: Spoken and Written
▶ *Main Idea:* The early disciples spoke and wrote the good news.
▶ *Suggested Teaching Aim:* To lead adults to describe how the good news was spoken and written.

A TEACHING OUTLINE

---

1. Writing the Good News (Luke 1:1–4)
2. Good News of Salvation (1 Cor. 15:1–4)
3. Testimony of an Eyewitness (1 John 1:1–4)

Introduce the Bible Study
IN ADVANCE, make this poster and display it: *Gospel = Good News.*

Ask, What good news have you heard this week? Let several members share. Say, The word *gospel* literally means "good news." The gospel is the best "good news" we can hear. Four different men wrote down the good news of Jesus, and we call their accounts *Gospels*. Today we look at how one of these wrote his account of the good news.

Search for Biblical Truth
On a chalkboard or a large sheet of paper, write: *Why write the good news?* Ask members to turn to Luke 1:1–2 and find an answer to this question. (To record the account of eyewitnesses of Jesus' life.)

Prepare a brief lecture using the material in "Studying the Bible" to describe these four factors that ensured the accuracy of what eventually was written: (1) people of that day were much more skilled at remembering and retelling what they had heard; (2) the apostles were around to ensure the accuracy of the spoken message; (3) the New Testament books were written either by eyewitnesses or on the basis of the testimony of the eyewitnesses; (4) the Holy Spirit guided in all this.

Write, *Who wrote the Good News?* Ask members to look at Luke 1:3–4 and answer this question. (Luke—although the text does not mention his name.) Lecture briefly, describing these three facts about Luke's

Gospel: (1) Before writing, Luke made a careful study of the coming, ministry, teachings, death, and resurrection of Jesus; (2) Luke wrote a complete and orderly account of the events of the Gospel; (3) Luke wrote as a believer to affirm the certainty of the Christian good news.

Write, *What is the purpose of the Good News?* (Saves us.) Ask members to look at 1 Corinthians 15:1–2 and find an answer. Lecture briefly, using the material in "Studying the Bible" to show how the Letters were written before the Gospels. Consider using the Time Line.

Write, *What is the Good News?* (Christ died, was buried, rose again.) Ask members to look at 1 Corinthians 15:3–4 and find an answer. Use the material in "Studying the Bible" to explain these three statements.

Write, *What was the Good News based on?* (Eyewitness accounts.) Ask members to look at 1 John 1:1–2 and answer the question. Use the parallel statements in "Studying the Bible" to compare the prologues to the Gospel of John (1:1–18) and 1 John (1:1–4). Point out that both prologues emphasize two things: (1) the eternal Word who was with the Father and (2) the reality of His incarnation. Ask, What evidence did John give in verse 1 that Jesus was truly human? (Believers had heard, seen, and touched Him.)

Write, *What was the purpose of the testimony of the eyewitnesses to the Good News?* Lecture briefly, describing the three words that define the purposes: (1) Life, (2) fellowship, (3) joy.

IN ADVANCE, write the four "Summary of Bible Truths" on four small strips of paper. Distribute these to four members and ask them to read the statements aloud to summarize the lesson.

Give the Truth a Personal Focus

Ask, How would you rank the good news of the gospel with the good news you have heard this week? Can you think of someone who needs to hear the good news of the gospel?

---

1. From a book entitled, *Not Ashamed of the Gospel,* p. 114.
2. H. C. Thiessen, *Lectures in Systematic Theology* (Grand Rapids: Eerdmans, 1956), 321.
3. Quoted in Charles Colson, *A Dangerous Grace* (Dallas: Word, 1994), 26.
4. *Fort Worth Star-Telegram,* October 30, 1959, Evening Edition, p. 43.
5. Robert A. Baker, *A Summary of Christian History,* rev. ed. by John M. Landers (Nashville: Broadman & Holman, 1994), 8.

The Birth of Jesus

Background Passage: Luke 2:1–20
Focal Passage: Luke 2:1–17

Matthew 1–2 and Luke 1–2 contain the only Gospel accounts of Jesus' birth and childhood. Luke 2:1–20 is the most complete and familiar Gospel account of the birth of Jesus. Although only one verse mentions the birth itself, the messages of the angels proclaim the meaning of that event.

▶**Study Aim:** *To celebrate Christmas consistently with the words of the angels and the responses of the shepherds.*

STUDYING THE BIBLE

OUTLINE AND SUMMARY
  I. **Circumstances of Jesus' Birth (Luke 2:1–7)**
     1. **Historical setting (2:1–2)**
     2. **Mary and Joseph (2:3–5)**
     3. **Laid in a manger (2:6–7)**
 II. **Angels' Words and Shepherds' Responses (Luke 2:8–20)**
     1. **Angel appears to shepherds (2:8–9)**
     2. **Angel's good news (2:10–12)**
     3. **Heavenly praises (2:13–14)**
     4. **Shepherds' responses (2:15–20)**

God used the taxation decree of the Roman emperor to accomplish His purposes (2:1–2). Mary and Joseph went from Nazareth to Bethlehem, Joseph's ancestral city (2:3–5). Jesus was laid in a manger after His birth (2:6–7). An angel appeared to shepherds (2:8–9). The angel announced good news of the Savior, Christ the Lord (2:10–12). A heavenly host praised God for bringing glory to Himself and peace to people (2:13–14). After the shepherds saw the baby, they told what the angels had announced to them (2:15–20).

I. Circumstances of Jesus' Birth (Luke 2:1–7)

5

1. Historical setting (2:1–2)

1 And it came to pass in those days, that there went out a decree from Caesar Augustus, that all the world should be taxed.

2 (And this taxing was first made when Cyrenius was governor of Syria.)

Caesar Augustus was the first emperor of the Roman Empire. He ruled from 31 B.C. until A.D. 14. Since all the civilized world was in the Roman Empire, Augustus had the authority to issue a decree for all to pay a special tax. Quirinius (Cyrenius) had some ruling function in the province of Syria, the larger province of which Judea was a part.

Luke went out of his way to include these notes about historical settings in Luke 1:5; 2:1; and 3:1. He seems to have had at least two reasons for doing this. First of all, he wanted to anchor the account of Jesus' birth, ministry, death, and resurrection in history. These were real events that took place at certain times in human history.

Luke also wanted to show that God moves in the affairs of nations to accomplish His own sovereign purposes. Centuries before Caesar Augustus, God had promised that the Messiah would be born in Bethlehem (Mic. 5:2; Matt. 2:4–6). Yet Joseph and Mary were residents of Nazareth, many miles from Bethlehem. God used the decree of the emperor in distant Rome to send Joseph and Mary to Bethlehem at just the right time for Jesus to be born.

2. Mary and Joseph (2:3–5)

3 And all went to be taxed, every one into his own city.

4 And Joseph also went up from Galilee, out of the city of Nazareth, into Judaea, unto the city of David, which is called, Bethlehem (because he was of the house and lineage of David:)

5 To be taxed with Mary his espoused wife, being great with child.

Bethlehem was the birthplace and ancestral home of David. Because Joseph was a descendant of David, he was required to journey to Bethlehem to be enrolled for the tax. Ordinarily a wife was not legally required to register for such a tax. Why then did Mary go with Joseph? She was soon to have a child, and such a long trip would be hard on her. The trip from Nazareth to Bethlehem was about ninety miles, mostly uphill. Mary may have gone because the unusual circumstances of her pregnancy were a subject of hostile gossip in the little town of Nazareth. Also, she knew her time was near, and she wanted to be with Joseph when the baby came.

Luke 1:26–35 has already recounted the angel's announcement to Mary that she would have a son who would be conceived by the Holy Spirit. At that time, she was a virgin "espoused to a man whose name was Joseph" (Luke 1:27). The word *espoused* means "engaged." Jewish engagements of that day were binding arrangements that could be broken only by divorce, but the engaged couple did not live together until after they were married. Matthew 1:18–25 tells how the Lord informed Joseph of the miracle of a child to be born to Mary. Joseph married her, but they did not live as husband and wife until after Jesus was born (Matt. 1:24–25).

3. Laid in a manger (2:6–7)

6 And so it was, that, while they were there, the days were accomplished that she should be delivered,

7 And she brought forth her firstborn son, and wrapped him in swaddling clothes and laid him in a manger; because there was no room for them in the inn.

No mention is made of a midwife; therefore, Mary herself wrapped the infant in the clothes. She laid him in a manger, a feeding trough for animals. This may have been in a stable, or it may have been in a house that kept animals under the same roof with the family—although in separate parts of the house.

The words "no room for them in the inn" need not mean that they were indifferently turned away. Possibly, the place with the manger was the only kind of place that ensured the privacy needed for the birth of a baby.

Throughout the biblical narratives of the events surrounding the birth of Jesus are signs that heaven reached down to touch earth. Some of the signs are obviously heavenly; some of the settings are very much of the earth. For example, Jesus was miraculously conceived within the womb of Mary; however, the process of His being born was a real birth. Other earthly-heavenly combinations include angels speaking to shepherds and wise men following a miraculous star.

II. Angels' Words and Shepherds' Responses (Luke 2:8–20)

1. Angel appears to shepherds (2:8–9)

8 And there were in the same country shepherds abiding in the field, keeping watch over their flock by night.

9 And, lo, the angel of the Lord came upon them, and the glory of the Lord shone round about them: and they were sore afraid.

Angels performed key roles in the events of Luke 1–2. An angel appeared to Zechariah (Luke 1:11–20) and to Mary (Luke 1:26–37). The initial responses of Zechariah and Mary was the same kind of fear that the shepherds felt (Luke 1:12, 29). The angel was accompanied by a shining light that represented the majestic splendor of God.

Shepherds have a mixed reputation in the Bible. David was a shepherd (1 Sam. 16:11; 17:34), Psalm 23 speaks of God as our Shepherd, and Jesus spoke of Himself as the Good Shepherd (John 10:11–18). However, shepherds were considered outcasts by respectable first-century Jews. Their wandering mode of living prevented them from performing many of the religious rituals. They also had a reputation as thieves. Therefore, the angel's appearance to moral and spiritual outcasts is significant. This shows that these were the kind of people whom Jesus came to save.

2. Angel's good news (2:10–12)

10 And the angel said unto them, Fear not: for behold, I bring you good tidings of great joy, which shall be to all people.

11 For unto you is born this day in the city of David a Saviour, which is Christ the Lord.

12 And this shall be a sign unto you; Ye shall find the babe wrapped in swaddling clothes, lying in a manger.

As in earlier appearances, the angel's first words were "fear not" (Luke 1:13, 30). Then the angel announced good news to the shepherds. The Greek word for "bring . . . good tidings" is the word that means "preach the good news (gospel)." The news would bring "great joy." Both "joy" and "peace" (2:14) are associated with the coming of Christ.

The good news was for "all people." This included the outcasts of Jewish society, and it included people of all nations. In Luke's second volume, the Book of Acts, he showed how God's Spirit broke through national, racial, and geographical barriers to tell the good news of salvation in Jesus Christ. In Matthew 2, those who saw and followed the star were Gentiles—foreshadowing the many Gentiles who would eventually follow Jesus as Savior and Lord.

The angel used three titles for Jesus that show why His coming was good news for all people. "Saviour" was a common title of the day for earthly benefactors. Caesar Augustus, for example, was often called a "savior" of humanity. However, the angel spoke of the Savior from sin and death (Matt. 1:21; John 4:42).

"Christ" is the Greek word for Messiah, the anointed King for whom the Jews had waited so long. Jesus is the fulfillment of God's promise to David (2 Sam. 7:12–16). As we saw in Matthew 16:13–26, Jesus was not the kind of Messiah many expected; He came to suffer, die, and be raised from the dead.

"Lord" is a title of reverence and deity (John 20:28). "Jesus Christ is Lord" became a basic confession for early Christians (Acts 2:36; Rom. 10:9–10; Phil. 2:9–11; 3:20).

The "sign" of verse 11 was to be a sign to the shepherds that the angel spoke the truth.

3. Heavenly praises (2:13–14)

13 And suddenly there was with the angel a multitude of the heavenly host praising God, and saying,

14 Glory to God in the highest, and on earth peace, good will toward men.

The heavenly host announced glory to God and peace to humanity. "Glory" represents the majestic splendor of God. The coming of Christ was to glorify God. God's glory was manifest in His Son (John 1:14; Heb. 1:3).

Verse 14 promises that the ultimate result of the coming of the Savior will be peace to people on earth. The word translated "good will" actually refers not to a part of the gift along with peace but to the peace that is bestowed as a gift of God's grace or good will toward humanity. Jesus brings peace with God and with one another, and His ultimate purpose is everlasting peace.

4. Shepherds' responses (2:15–20)

15 And it came to pass, as the angels were gone away from them into heaven, the shepherds said one to another, Let us now go even unto Bethlehem, and see this thing which is come to pass, which the Lord hath made known unto us.

16 And they came with haste, and found Mary, and Joseph, and the babe lying in a manger.

17 And when they had seen it, they made known abroad the saying which was told them concerning this child.

The shepherds were not forced to go to Bethlehem. They decided for themselves to go. Then as now, the decision to seek the Savior is a personal choice. Imagine what a tragedy it would have been if they had decided not to go or had put it off until it was too late!

When they got to Bethlehem, they found just what the angel had described as a sign that all he told them was true. Therefore, the shepherds left and spread the good news they had heard from the angels. The people who heard them wondered at what the shepherds told them (2:18). The shepherds returned to their work praising and glorifying God (2:20).

Isn't it striking that these lowly shepherds were chosen by God to hear the first Christmas sermon and the first Christmas carol? Even more amazing, they became the first humans to tell the good news of Jesus Christ, the Savior of the world!

Mary treasured and remembered all these things (2:19). She was probably Luke's eyewitness source for much of this part of the Gospel (Luke 1:1–4).

SUMMARY OF BIBLE TRUTHS

1. God works in the affairs of nations to accomplish His purposes.
2. The birth of Jesus was to a virgin, but it was a real birth, testifying to His full deity and full humanity.
3. Jesus came as Savior for sinners and for people of all nations.
4. Jesus revealed the glory of God and offered peace and joy to people who receive Him.
5. God can use the most unlikely people as witnesses of the good news.

APPLYING THE BIBLE

1. Christmas makes us sing! I love the story about the boy who was lustily singing Christmas hymns one February night in his bedroom. When his friend asked him why, he said that he had caught a cold in December and couldn't sing them then! Make a list of three well-known Christmas hymns sung in your church, and indicate why it is fitting to sing them all year long.

2. Two themes of the angels' song. The angels' song had two main themes:

(1)   God is glorious, and
(2)   Christmas has a profound effect on earth.

As you sing Christmas songs this year, watch for those two themes.

3. Why do I love Christmas? A cartoon writer, at Christmas time, put this thought into the mind of a baby in a crib: "I sure do love Christmas. Boy, do I love Christmas! I don't know what it's all about, but I sure do love it!" Why do we love Christmas?

4. God uses unlikely people to witness the good news. During World War II, Jews around Wilna, Poland, were desperate to escape Hitler's troops. Some of these Jews hid out in a cemetery. One cold night, in a grave, a young Jewish woman gave birth to a boy, attended only by an eighty-year-old gravedigger. Upon the child's birth, the gravedigger bowed his head and softly prayed, "Father, thank You for the Messiah born to us this night. Who else but the Messiah could be born in a grave?" The old man was wrong about the identity of the child, but he knew the Old Testament truth that the Messiah must suffer and die for His people. Even at Christmas, we must never forget that the cross was always in the Christ child's future.

5. Christ in Christmas. C. S. Lewis wrote, "My brother heard a woman on a 'bus say, as the 'bus passed a church with a Crib outside it, 'Oh, Lor'! They bring religion into everything. Look—they're dragging it even into Christmas now!'" Lewis was describing what happened in England. What are the evidences that the same misunderstanding of Christmas occurs in our country?

6. The miracle of Christmas. It is impossible for anybody to understand Christmas apart from the sheer miracle of it all. There is a natural tendency to "horizontalize" life—to explain it in purely natural terms. Some theologians even explain away the miracle of the virgin birth of Christ and raise objections to this New Testament teaching. But C. S. Lewis put it well when he wrote: "All the essentials of Hinduism would, I think, remain unimpaired if you subtracted the miraculous, and the same is almost true of Mohammedanism. But you cannot do that with Christianity. It is precisely the story of a great Miracle. A naturalistic Christianity leaves out all that is specifically Christian."[2]

TEACHING THE BIBLE

▶ *Main Idea:* The angels' words and the shepherds' responses provide a way to celebrate Christmas.

▶ *Suggested Teaching Aim:* To lead adults to celebrate Christmas consistent with the angels' words and the shepherds' responses.

A TEACHING OUTLINE

The Birth of Jesus
1. *Circumstances of Jesus' Birth (Luke 2:1–7)*
2. *Angels' Words and Shepherds' Responses (Luke 2:8–20)*

Introduce the Bible Study
Use "Why do I love Christmas?" in "Applying the Bible" to introduce the lesson. Let members share why they love Christmas. Say: Today's lesson will help us to celebrate Christmas consistent with the angels' words and the shepherds' responses.

Search for Biblical Truth
On a chalkboard or a large sheet of paper write: **Earthly** and **Heavenly** at the top of two columns. Leave space to write members' responses beneath each word.

Ask members to listen for evidences of earthly and heavenly events about the birth of Jesus as a volunteer reads Luke 2:1–2. Ask members to share what they found. (Members may find many evidences, but consider these: **Earthly:** taxes, Caesar, Quirinius; **Heavenly:** God promised Messiah would be born in Bethlehem.)

Ask members to listen for evidences of earthly and heavenly events about the birth of Jesus, as a volunteer reads Luke 2:3–5. (**Heavenly:** God used a decree to get Mary and Joseph to Bethlehem.) Use a map of the New Testament world to show that the trip was about ninety miles, mostly uphill. Explain the meaning of the word *espoused*.

Ask members to listen for evidences of earthly and heavenly events about the birth of Jesus, as a volunteer reads Luke 2:6–7. (**Earthly:** human birth, manger, swaddling clothes; **Heavenly:** miraculous conception, delivered Messiah in Bethlehem.) Explain "no room for them in the inn."

Ask members to listen for evidences of earthly and heavenly events about the birth of Jesus, as a volunteer reads Luke 2:8–9. (**Earthly:** shepherds, sheep; **Heavenly:** angels, light.)

DISCUSS: How have you or your church shared the good news with social outcasts recently?

Ask members to listen for evidences of earthly and heavenly events about the birth of Jesus, as a volunteer reads Luke 2:10–12. (**Heavenly:** angel's announcement, Savior born, sign.) Explain the three titles the angel used for Jesus: Savior, Christ, and Lord.

Ask members to listen for evidences of earthly and heavenly events about the birth of Jesus, as a volunteer reads Luke 2:13–14. (**Heavenly:** multitude of angels singing.) Ask, According to this passage, what is the ultimate result of the coming of the Savior? (Peace.)

DISCUSS: What can you do to bring peace in the world in which you live?

Ask members to listen for evidences of earthly and heavenly events about the birth of Jesus, as a volunteer reads Luke 2:15–17. (**Earthly:** went to the manger, told people about Jesus; **Heavenly:** found Baby who was the Messiah; first witnesses to tell good news of Jesus.)

DISCUSS: Why does God leave it to each person to seek or not to seek the Christ child?

Give the Truth a Personal Focus

Ask, How can we celebrate Christmas consistent with the angels' words and the shepherds' responses? Refer to the list of **Earthly** and **Heavenly** evidences. Say: Much of the heavenly evidence is earthly evidence used for a heavenly purpose. Suggest that this is often the way God works today. Ask members to list some earthly events or activities that God could use to help them celebrate Christmas consistent with the angels' words and the shepherds' responses.

Close by reading the words to the hymn "Joy to the World."

---

1. C. S. Lewis, *Letters to an American Lady,* ed., Clyde Kilby (Grand Rapids: Eerdmans, 1967), 80.

2. C. S. Lewis, *Miracles* (New York: Macmillan, 1960), 68.

Christ's Presence Continues

Background Passage: Luke 24:13–53
Focal Passage: Luke 24:36–53

This study of Luke 24 marks the climax in the first unit in a survey of the New Testament. We have focused on "The Good News of Jesus Christ" from both the Gospels and the Letters. Luke 24 is Luke's account of the resurrection appearances and Jesus' ascension.

▶**Study Aim:** To describe what the early followers of Jesus experienced and learned during the appearances of the Lord.

STUDYING THE BIBLE

OUTLINE AND SUMMARY

    I. **Appearing on the Emmaus Road (Luke 24:13–32)**
        1. **Two followers joined by unrecognized Jesus (24:13–16)**
        2. **Their confusion and despair (24:17–24)**
        3. **Words of Jesus to them (24:25–27)**
        4. **Recognizing the risen Lord (24:28–32)**
    II. **Appearing to the Apostles (Luke 24:33–49)**
        1. **Appearance to Simon (24:33–35)**
        2. **Reality of Jesus' bodily resurrection (24:36–43)**
        3. **Opening the Scriptures (24:44–47)**
        4. **Commissioning the apostles as witnesses (24:48–49)**
    III. **Ascending into Heaven (Luke 24:50–53)**

Jesus was not recognized by two followers on the road to Emmaus (24:13–16). They told Him of their dashed hopes as a result of the Crucifixion (24:17–24). Jesus opened the Scriptures to them (24:25–27). After they recognized Him, they remembered how their hearts had burned (24:28–32). Returning to Jerusalem, they were told that the Lord had appeared to Simon (24:33–35). When Jesus appeared among the apostles, the Lord proved He was not merely a spirit (24:36–43). Jesus explained how the Scriptures predicted His death and resurrection, forgiveness of sins based on repentance, and a mission to all nations (24:44–47). The Lord commissioned the apostles as His witnesses and told them to wait for the promised power (24:48–49). After Jesus' ascension, His followers returned to Jerusalem rejoicing (24:50–53).

I. Appearing on the Emmaus Road (Luke 24:13–32)

1. Two followers joined by unrecognized Jesus (24:13–16)

Two followers of Jesus (one named Cleopas, 24:18) were walking from Jerusalem to Emmaus, about seven miles away (24:13). The two were discussing recent events when Jesus joined them; however, they were kept from recognizing Him (24:14–15).

2. Their confusion and despair (24:17–24)

When Jesus asked what they were discussing, they were surprised that even a stranger in Jerusalem had not heard about Jesus of Nazareth (24:17–18). They told how many had regarded Jesus as "a prophet mighty in deed and word" (24:19). They told how the religious leaders had brought about His condemnation and crucifixion (24:20). They testified that they had hoped that Jesus was the Messiah who would redeem Israel (24:21). Then the two reported the strange events of that day. When women went to the tomb, the body was gone; but the women reported seeing a vision of angels claiming that Jesus was alive (24:22–23). Some men also found the tomb empty (24:24).

3. Words of Jesus to them (24:25–27)

The unrecognized Jesus called them "slow of heart to believe all that the prophets have spoken" (24:25). He asked if it was not necessary for the Messiah "to have suffered these things, and to enter into his glory" (24:26). Then He began with the books of Moses and explained the Scriptures concerning the Messiah (24:27).

4. Recognizing the risen Lord (24:28–32)

When they reached Emmaus, the two insisted that the stranger stay with them (24:28–29). As they prepared to eat, the stranger blessed the bread (24:30). Then they were able to recognize Jesus, but He vanished from their sight (24:31). They agreed that their hearts had burned within them as He opened the Scriptures to them (24:32).

II. Appearing to the Apostles (Luke 24:33–49)

1. Appearance to Simon (24:33–35)

The two followers rushed back to Jerusalem (24:33). The apostles told them, "The Lord is risen indeed, and hath appeared to Simon" (24:34). Then the two told of their experiences (24:35).

2. Reality of Jesus' bodily resurrection (24:36–43)

36 And as they thus spake, Jesus himself stood in the midst of them, and saith unto them, Peace be unto you.

37 But they were terrified and affrighted, and supposed that they had seen a spirit.

38 And he said unto them, Why are ye troubled? and why do thoughts arise in your hearts?

39 Behold my hands and my feet, that it is I myself: handle me, and see; for a spirit hath not flesh and bones, as ye see me have.

40 And when he had thus spoken, he shewed them his hands and his feet.

41 And while they yet believed not for joy, and wondered, he said unto them, Have ye here any meat?

42 And they gave him a piece of a broiled fish, and of an honeycomb.

43 And he took it, and did eat before them.

All the biblical records emphasize that the followers of Jesus were not expecting Him to be raised from the dead. When the women reported an empty tomb and angels saying Jesus was alive, the apostles called such reports "idle tales" (Luke 24:11). Even after the risen Lord had appeared on the Emmaus Road and to Simon, they were terrified when He appeared among them. They thought they were seeing only a spirit. They had troubled and doubting thoughts.

Jesus, therefore, showed them that it was truly He and that His was a body, not just a spirit. First, he challenged them to look at and to touch His hands and feet. Then He ate with them. Even as they began to rejoice and believe, they still wondered. They couldn't believe what their senses were showing them to be true.

One purpose of the resurrection appearances of Jesus was to prove the reality of His bodily resurrection. During forty days, the risen Lord appeared to many groups and individuals "by many infallible proofs" that He had been raised from the dead (Acts 1:3). The basis for the apostles' testimony to this reality was that they saw Him alive. The empty tomb had other possible explanations, but the many appearances showed them that this was Jesus.

3. Opening the Scriptures (24:44–47)

44 And he said unto them, These are the words which I spake unto you, while I was yet with you, that all things must be fulfilled, which were written in the law of Moses, and in the prophets, and in the psalms, concerning me.

45 Then opened he their understanding, that they might understand the scriptures,

46 And said unto them, Thus it is written, and thus it behoved Christ to suffer, and to rise from the dead the third day;

47 And that repentance and remission of sins should be preached in his name among all nations, beginning at Jerusalem.

Scholars debate whether verses 44–49 describe events of that first Sunday evening or of a later appearance. Many believe that these words were spoken near the end of the forty days, perhaps even at the appearance just before His ascension. At some time during His appearances, the risen Lord opened the Scriptures to His followers. Verse 44 lists all three divisions of the Hebrew Bible: Law, Prophets, and Writings. Jesus opened their understanding so they could see how the Scriptures predicted His suffering, death, and resurrection.

The apostles knew the Scriptures, but they had accepted traditional interpretations of the Messiah. These interpretations emphasized the passages that presented the Messiah as a mighty King, but did not see passages like Isaiah 53 as referring to the Messiah. Luke 24 does not list specific passages that Jesus opened to them. However, we can discover what they were by studying the Old Testament passages quoted in the New Testament.

Jesus also showed how the Scriptures predicted that the Messiah's suffering and resurrection would involve an offer of forgiveness of sins in His name based on repentance, and that this forgiveness was to be for people of all nations, not just for the Jews. Thus, verse 47 focuses on the message of salvation and on the scope of this good news. Repentance and faith are two sides of the response that results in forgiveness of sins (Acts 20:21). Repentance is turning from sins, and faith is turning in trust to the Lord.

The apostles had fewer problems accepting this than they did the fact that this message was for all nations. The book of Acts shows the struggle among two groups of Jewish believers. One group wanted to confine the good news to Jews or to those willing to become Jews. Others—like Stephen, Philip, and Paul—insisted that salvation by grace through faith was for all people.

In all the Gospels and the book of Acts, the final marching orders of the Lord were to take the good news to all people (Matt. 28:18–20; Mark 16:15; John 20:21; Acts 1:8). If a loved one made a deathbed request, most of us would do everything in our power to do what we were asked. The Lord of glory has commissioned us to do the thing closest to His heart—that for which He gave His life. Why are we so slow to obey Him?

4. Commissioning the apostles as witnesses (24:48–49)

48 And ye are witnesses of these things.

49 And, behold, I send the promise of my Father upon you: but tarry ye in the city of Jerusalem, until ye be endued with power from on high.

Acts 1:22 states the qualifications for an apostle:
- one who had been with Jesus from the beginning of His ministry,
- a witness of His resurrection, and
- one appointed by Jesus as an apostle.

Here is the commissioning service for the apostles. Paul later claimed apostleship based on meeting the last two qualifications (1 Cor. 15:8–10; Gal. 1:11–2:10).

As we have noted in earlier lessons, the New Testament is the written record of the testimony of these apostolic witnesses. Every Christian is a witness, but only an apostle could bear eyewitness testimony to the risen Lord. Our testimony is based on believing their witness and having experienced forgiveness and new life in the Spirit of the Lord.

One purpose of the forty days was to prepare believers for a new way of relating to the Lord Jesus. He was not with them all during the forty days, but appeared only from time to time. He was training them to be aware of His presence even when they did not see Him. Thus, He reminded them that they would perform their task as witnesses in the power of the Spirit promised by the Father. Based on Acts 2:16–21, the promise of the Spirit was the one in Joel 2:28–32.

III. Ascending into Heaven (Luke 24:50–53)

50 And he led them out as far as to Bethany, and he lifted up his hands, and blessed them.

51 And it came to pass, while he blessed them, he was parted from them, and carried up into heaven.

52 And they worshipped him, and returned to Jerusalem with great joy:

53 And were continually in the temple, praising and blessing God. Amen.

Acts 1:9–11 also describes the ascension of Jesus. What was the purpose of His ascension?

1. The Ascension was part of the divine exaltation of Jesus that began with the Resurrection. It served as the climax and guarantee of the success of Jesus' mission as Savior.
2. The Ascension assures us of Christ's presence at the right hand of God as our mediator and intercessor (Heb. 7:25).
3. The Ascension guarantees the continuation of His redemptive work through His Spirit with us. The Lord Jesus is both at God's right hand and also in our hearts by His Spirit (Rom. 8:9).
4. The Ascension points to the sure return of the Lord and the final subjection of all people and things to Him (Acts 1:9–11; Phil. 2:9–11).

This explains how the followers of Jesus could return from the Ascension rejoicing. When they had lost the physical presence of Jesus through His death, they had been paralyzed with fears and despair. Now, however, even though the Lord's earthly presence was withdrawn, they could rejoice.

SUMMARY OF BIBLE TRUTHS

1. The appearances of the risen Lord showed the reality of His bodily resurrection from the dead.
2. The Old Testament foretold the death and resurrection of Jesus and forgiveness in His name offered to all nations.
3. The apostles were commissioned as special eyewitnesses, but we are all to be witnesses.
4. The final marching orders of the Lord were to take the good news to all nations.
5. The Lord Jesus continues to guide and empower His people to fulfill that commission.

APPLYING THE BIBLE

1. Jesus is walking with us. A boy of about seven once decided to run away from home. He packed a small bag, slipped out the back door, and began to walk down a country road away from his home. Presently, darkness fell and fear did too. As he approached a state of panic, he heard sounds from a line of trees along the roadside and saw a thrilling sight: His father was walking onto the roadway. His father embraced him and then told his son that he had been walking along with him, though all the while out of sight and sound. That is what the Emmaus disciples experienced. And that is what we experience.

2. Somebody's listening! Two of my nephews and I were soundly disciplined—in a real woodshed! It was my first cigarette (and my last!). We were caught by a tattletale younger sister, and we paid the price. After a sound spanking, the three of us sat and commiserated, licking our wounds. I said, "I'm never going to smoke again in my whole life!" My younger nephew agreed, but my older nephew didn't see it that way. Defiantly, he pronounced his intent to smoke whenever and wherever he chose. Imagine his pain—and my pleasure—when his father (my surrogate father) stepped out from behind a door, from which position he had heard the entire conversation. The moral? Somebody's listening!

3. We are important to God. What amazing condescension! I have often been amazed that Jesus took so much time with two apparently run-of-the-mill disciples. He often did that. Remember His spending time with Nicodemus (John 3:1f) and the rich young ruler (Luke 18:18f), and the woman healed of the issue of blood—and the daughter of Jairus in the same story (Luke 8:41f), and so many others. G. K. Chesterton once said that the most unbelievable truth in the entire universe is that *I matter*. Those two disciples did, and Jesus' presence proved it—and did so beautifully.

4. Everything depends on the Resurrection. If the Resurrection happened, we must interpret all things in the light of that fact. If it didn't happen, we must interpret all things in the light of that fact. Dr. Earl Guinn, former president of Lousiana College, once said, in an Easter sermon, what we all instinctively know: "If Jesus did not rise from the dead, nothing really matters. But if He did, nothing *else* matters."

5. Christ's resurrection is the watershed. On Cut Bank Pass in Glacier National Park, three brooks are so close together that a person can pour water into all three by taking only a few steps. One brook carries water to Hudson Bay in northern Canada, another to the Pacific Ocean, and the third into the Gulf of Mexico. Some call this point "the top of the North American continent." Like this natural watershed, the resurrection of Christ is the moral and theological watershed for all who travel through history.

6. Christ's resurrection makes the difference. Albert Mohler writes, "The French positivist philosopher Auguste Comte once told Thomas Carlyle that he planned to start a new religion to replace Christianity. 'Very good,' replied Carlyle. 'All you have to do is be crucified, rise the third day, and get the world to believe you are still alive. Then your new religion will have a chance,'"[1] Because of the logic of that statement, Easter stands as a mighty judgment against every other religion ever known on the earth!

7. Nobody to thank. Steve Brown tells of a man who felt he had to give up his Christian faith and became an atheist. Years later, the atheist's beloved wife died, and he wrote a letter to his friend about his immense sense of loss. He began the letter by writing, "I thank . . ." But then he realized, if God didn't exist and if Christ hadn't risen, he had no one to thank for the gift of the woman he had loved so much. With tears streaming down his face, the man wrote these words: "I thank something that I loved her as heartily as I knew how to love." Among other things, prayer is profoundly affected if Christ is risen! The early disciples, in our study, spoke with a living Christ. And so can we!²

8. For thought and study:

▶ Is Christ listening to our conversations?

▶ How would our conversations change if we acknowledged His presence in every such setting?

▶ The basic problem of these two disciples was not unbelief; it was ignorance of the Scriptures. Is it possible to understand the meaning of events around us without a thorough knowledge of the Scriptures?

▶ If Christ made Himself known to us and corrected our theology, what are the precise issues, in your estimation, He would focus on? Where have we most misinterpreted Him and His word?

TEACHING THE BIBLE

▶ *Main Idea:* The early followers of Jesus learned from His appearances that Jesus was alive.

▶ *Suggested Teaching Aim*: To lead adults to describe how the early disciples knew Jesus was alive.

A TEACHING OUTLINE

Christ's Presence Continues

1. *Appearing on the Emmaus Road (Luke 24:13–32)*
2. *Appearing to the Apostles (Luke 24:33–49)*
3. *Ascending to Heaven (Luke 24:50–53)*

Introduce the Bible Study

As members enter, greet them with "Merry Christmas and Happy Easter!" Sing (or read aloud) "Christ the Lord Is Risen Today." Then ask: How do you feel about hearing references to Easter only two days after Christmas? Say: Today we conclude the first unit of our study on the New Testament. If you made the unit poster, point out the title of the unit poster.

Search for Biblical Truth

Since the lesson jumps from the birth of Jesus to His resurrection, it will help to establish the context of the lesson. Enlist two readers to read alternately the eight summary statements in the Outline and Summary.

Make a teaching outline poster by copying the three points of the teaching outline on a large sheet of paper. Using the material in "Studying the Bible," briefly summarize the first point. Ask a volunteer to read Luke 24:36–43. Ask, What biblical evidence can you cite that Jesus' followers expected Him to rise from the dead? (None.) What evidence can you cite that indicates their disbelief and surprise that He rose from the dead? (Called reports "idle tales," terrified when He appeared to them, thought they were seeing a spirit.)

Ask: What did Jesus do to show them that He was a body and not just a spirit? (Showed His hands and feet, ate with them.) How were these proofs more convincing than the empty tomb? (Empty tomb could be explained away; His appearances could not.)

Ask a volunteer to read 24:44–47. Ask: What Scriptures do you think He referred to in His conversation with His followers (24:44–45)? (Possibly Isa. 53 was one.) On a chalkboard write *Forgiveness = repentance and faith.* Explain that repentance is turning from sins and faith is turning in trust to the Lord. Ask: What in verse 47 did the apostles have the most trouble accepting? (Jesus' message was for all people.)

Ask members to look at 24:48–49 and identify two statements Jesus made about the disciples: (They are His witnesses, and He will send the Spirit.) Ask: Do these two statements apply to us? (Yes.)

Point to the third outline point. Ask members to look at 24:50–53. Ask, What was the purpose of the Ascension? (1) Served as climax and guarantee of the success of Jesus' mission as Savior; (2) assures us of Christ's presence at the right hand of God as our Mediator and Intercessor; (3) guarantees the continuation of His redemptive work through His Spirit; (4) points to the sure return of the Lord and the final subjection of all people and things to Him.

Read this statement: "When they had lost the physical presence of Jesus through His death, they had been paralyzed with fears and despair. Now, however, even though the Lord's earthly presence was withdrawn, they could rejoice."

Read the five "Summary of Bible Truths" statements to emphasize the teachings of the lesson.

Give the Truth a Personal Focus

Ask, How did the early disciples know Jesus was alive? List their reasons on a chalkboard. Ask: Are these reasons still valid today? Why?

---

1. R. Albert Mohler in *Christian Index,* April 12, 1990, p. 2.
2. Quoted from *Key Life* (March–April 1994).

People of Love

Background Passages: Mark 12:28–34; Luke 6:27–36; John 13:31–35

Focal Passages: Mark 12:28–34; Luke 6:27–31; John 13:34–35

During the next four weeks, our survey of the New Testament will focus on four key themes of Jesus' teaching. Appropriately, we begin with the central theme of His life and teaching: love. Passages from three of the Gospels have been chosen to illustrate the scope of Christian love. Christians are to love not only one another but also all people (neighbors), including enemies.

▶**Study Aim:** *To identify similarities and differences between love for neighbors, enemies, and fellow Christians.*

STUDYING THE BIBLE

OUTLINE AND SUMMARY

    I. **Love Your Neighbors (Mark 12:28–34)**
        1. **The first commandment (12:28–31))**
        2. **Not far from the kingdom (12:32–34)**
   II. **Love Your Enemies (Luke 6:27–36)**
        1. **Do good to your enemies (6:27–30)**
        2. **Practice the Golden Rule (6:31)**
        3. **Love as God loves (6:32–36)**
 III. **Love One Another (John 13:31–35)**
        1. **Father and Son glorified (13:31–33)**
        2. **A new commandment (13:34–35)**

When a scribe asked Jesus to name the first commandment, Jesus cited total love for God and love for one's neighbor (Mark 12:28–31). When the scribe said this was more important than sacrifices, Jesus said that he was not far from the kingdom (Mark 12:32–34). Jesus commanded His followers to do good for those who hate and hurt them (Luke 6:27–30). Believers should practice the Golden Rule (Luke 6:31). Love for enemies is God's kind of self-giving love (Luke 6:32–36). The Father and Son were glorified in Jesus' death and resurrection (John 13:31–33). Jesus gave a new commandment for believers to love one another as He had loved them (John 13:34–35).

I. Love Your Neighbors (Mark 12:28–34)

1. The first commandment (12:28–31)

> **28 And one of the scribes came, and having heard them reasoning together, and perceiving that he had answered them well, asked him, Which is the first commandment of all?**

The setting for this incident was during the last week of Jesus' life as He was teaching in the temple. Much of His teaching consisted of answers to questions, mostly trick questions (Mark 12:14–27). A scribe who had observed all this then asked Jesus a question. The scribes were experts in the Jewish religious laws and traditions. Most of the scribes were hostile to Jesus; however, this unnamed scribe had an open mind toward Jesus and His teachings.

The question was one that he and other scribes often discussed. In their zeal to keep the Law, they had identified 613 laws; therefore, they discussed which of these many laws was first in importance.

29 And Jesus answered him, The first of all the commandments is, Hear, O Israel; The Lord our God is one Lord:

30 And thou shalt love the Lord thy God with all thy heart, and with all thy soul, and with all thy mind, and with all thy strength: this is the first commandment.

31 And the second is like, namely this, Thou shalt love thy neighbour as thyself. There is none other commandment greater than these.

Jesus answered the question by quoting a familiar Old Testament passage, Deuteronomy 6:4–5. This was a part of the Jewish *Shema,* which pious Jews recited daily. It contained their basic profession of faith in the Lord as the one true God, and it called for wholehearted love toward God. Love was not the usual word in the Old Testament to describe how to respond to God. More familiar words were "obey," "fear," "trust," "praise," and "worship." The use of the word *love* here reflects the emphasis in Deuteronomy on God's love for Israel (Deut. 4:37; 7:13; 10:15; 15:16).

To love God meant to show total devotion to Him alone. Since most of the ancient world worshiped many gods, they had to spread their devotion around. However, since the Israelites worshiped only one God, they were able to give total devotion to Him. This is the force of the four-fold repetition of "with all thy heart, . . . soul, . . . mind, . . . strength." They were to love God with all they had and were. Jesus said that this was the first commandment.

He added a second commandment that He considered inseparable from total devotion to God. He quoted Leviticus 19:18. Jesus said, "There is none other commandment greater than these." In the parallel passage in Matthew 22:40, Jesus added, "On these two commandments hang all the law and the prophets" (Matt. 22:40).

During Old Testament times, Leviticus 19:18 was limited to Israelites and resident aliens (Lev. 19:33–34). Jesus placed no limits on the definition of "neighbor." When someone asked, "Who is my neighbour?" Jesus told the story of the good Samaritan (Luke 10:29–37). All people are our neighbors, especially those in need.

2. Not far from the kingdom (12:32–34)

32 And the scribe said unto him, Well, Master, thou hast said the truth: for there is one God; and there is none other than he:

33 And to love him with all the heart, and with all the understanding, and with all the soul, and with all the strength, and

to love his neighbour as himself, is more than all whole burnt offerings and sacrifices.

34 And when Jesus saw that he answered discreetly, he said unto him, Thou art not far from the kingdom of God. And no man after that durst ask him any question.

This open-minded scribe recognized the truth in what Jesus said. He showed his insight by his remark in the last of verse 33. "Whole burnt offerings and sacrifices" were supposed to represent a worshiper's total dedication. The scribe realized that people could go through the motions of worship without really loving God totally and certainly without loving others as themselves. This was not a new insight. Many of the prophets had said as much (1 Sam. 15:22; Isa. 1:11–17; Hos. 6:6; Amos 5:21–24; Mic. 6:6–8).

Jesus recognized the wisdom of the scribe's response. Jesus commended the scribe by saying that he was not far from the kingdom. This didn't imply that he was in the kingdom, but it did say that he was near. It was a challenge to him to go ahead and enter by becoming a follower of Jesus. We don't know the scribe's response.

II. Love Your Enemies (Luke 6:27–36)

1. Do good to your enemies (6:27–30)

27 But I say unto you which hear, Love your enemies, do good to them which hate you,

28 Bless them that curse you, and pray for them which despitefully use you.

29 And unto him that smiteth thee on the one cheek offer also the other; and him that taketh away thy cloak forbid not to take thy coat also.

30 Give to every man that asketh of thee; and of him that taketh away thy goods ask them not again.

The heart of the passage is the command of Jesus for His followers to love their enemies. A more typical reaction, which is sometimes even sanctioned by religious people, is to hate one's enemies (Matt. 5:43). Jesus used three words to describe how enemies treat you: "hate," "curse," "despitefully use." The last of these means to "abuse," "manipulate," or "exploit." Christians are to "do good to," "bless," and "pray for" people who treat them in these hostile and harmful ways.

This points up a basic aspect of Christian love. *Christian love is doing good for others, regardless of your feelings toward them or their feelings and actions toward you.* In other words, Christian love is not a warm fuzzy feeling for others. It is doing good for them no matter how we feel about them. How else could anyone love his enemies?

Verses 29–30 give four illustrations of this principle. These are difficult verses at best; they are impossible and self-defeating if we take them as hard-and-fast rules. When you are hit on one cheek, this injures and insults you. The normal reaction is to strike back, but Jesus said to turn the other cheek. Jesus was countering the tendency to want to get even.

The other three illustrations have to do with possessions. Jesus said to give the thief more than he took and to give freely to the person who asks for a gift or a loan. Jesus' words are not laws to be obeyed in every circumstance. We are people with limited resources in a world of limitless needs. The normal human tendency is to grasp our own possessions and to seek restitution from those who take them from us. Jesus taught us to resist these natural tendencies and to be merciful and generous.

2. Practice the Golden Rule (6:31)

> **31 And as ye would that men should do to you, do ye also to them likewise.**

The Golden Rule is also found in Matthew 7:12. Many wise teachers had stated a negative version of this principle: Don't do to others what you don't want them to do to you. Jesus stated this principle positively. The negative rule requires no action. The priest and Levite in Jesus' story practiced the negative rule. The Samaritan practiced the Golden Rule (Luke 10:30–37).

The Golden Rule calls for three actions: (1) Put yourself in the other person's shoes; (2) ask yourself, "If I were that person, how would I want to be treated?" and (3) take the initiative in treating the person as you would want to be treated in his or her place.

3. Love as God loves (6:32–36)

Christian love is self-giving, not self-serving. Even sinners love people who love them, do good to people who do good to them, and lend to people who lend to them (6:32–34). Those who return good for evil show themselves to be children of God, because He is kind to the ungrateful and evil (6:35). Christians, therefore, are to be merciful as God is merciful (6:36).

III. Love One Another (John 13:31–35)

1. Father and Son glorified (John 13:31–33)

The Lord said that the time had come for the Father and Son to be glorified—through the Cross and the Resurrection (13:31–32). Jesus began the theme of His departure and return that continued throughout His farewell address in John 14–16.

2. A new commandment (John 13:34–35)

> **34 A new commandment I give unto you, That ye love one another; as I have loved you, that ye also love one another.**

> **35 By this shall all men know that ye are my disciples, if ye have love one to another.**

Not only are Christians to love all people; we are to love one another. Believers have been adopted as children into the family of the heavenly Father, in which all fellow believers are brothers and sisters in Christ. The mutual love from and for the Father obligates believers to do good for others who share that love.

In what sense is this a new commandment?

1. Jesus made love the primary Christian quality.
2. Jesus created a new family of faith and love.

3. Jesus provided the motive, model, and measure of this love by giving Himself for us.

We are to love one another as Christ loved us. His was a self-giving, sacrificial love. His love is the pattern and power for our love for one another. Christian husbands are to love their wives "as Christ also loved the church, and gave himself for it" (Eph. 5:25). Christians are to forgive "one another, even as God for Christ's sake hath forgiven us" (Eph. 4:32).

The world will recognize followers of Christ by their love for one another. At its best, Christian love captures the attention of an unbelieving world and points them to Christ. When we fail to show such love (as is all too often the case), no wonder the world pays no heed to messages about the love of God for a lost world!

Jesus called this a "commandment." We ought to feel brotherly love for other family members, but sometimes we don't get along with one another. Still we are commanded to do good for one another. The family of faith and love ought to provide the training ground for practicing Christian love toward outsiders. If we can't act in love toward fellow believers, how will we ever be able to love our enemies?

SUMMARY OF BIBLE TRUTHS

1. Christian love includes all people: fellow Christians, neighbors, even enemies.
2. Christian love means doing good for others, regardless of our feelings or of their hostile feelings and actions toward us.
3. Christian love involves self-giving, even sacrificial love—not self-seeking or reciprocal treatment of friends.
4. Christian love is motivated by and modeled after God's love for us and others.

APPLYING THE BIBLE

1. Love reaches out. "In France, during World War II, some men took the body of a buddy to a local cemetery. The priest would not let them bury their friend there because he was not a Catholic. The men buried their friend just outside the cemetery fence. The next day they could not find the grave. The priest explained, 'The first part of the night I stayed awake, sorry for what I had told you. The second part of the night I spent moving the fence.'" This is my favorite "love" story. It is a marvelous picture of how we should love the "outsider." It is also a marvelous picture of what Christ did for us—in love. He moved the fence and put us inside God's love!

2. Living together in love. Here's the problem:

To live above with those we love,
That will be glory;
But to live below with those we know,
That's another story.

In his poem "Locksley Hall Sixty Year After," Alfred, Lord Tennyson wrote:

> Love your enemy, bless your haters, said the Greatest of the
> great;
> Christian love among the Churches looked the twin of heathen
> hate.

3. Apply the Golden Rule to yourself. Robert Dean says, "The Golden Rule calls for three actions: (1) Put yourself in the other person's shoes; (2) ask yourself, 'If I were that person, how would I want to be treated?' and (3) take the initiative in treating the person as you would want to be treated in his or her place." For discussion, apply these suggestions in response to: (1) the person who is in poverty; (2) the person who has a different color of skin; (3) the person who has a debilitating and disfiguring disease; and (4) the person of old age.

4. Three Greek words are translated *love:*

1. Eros refers to sensual love. The Greek New Testament never used the word eros.

2. Philia refers to friendship or tender affection; it emphasizes a relationship in which both persons like some quality or qualities of, or feel a special affinity with, the other person.

3. Agape refers to Christian love, whether exercised toward other Christians or toward people in general. It is not an impulse from the feelings; it does not always run with the natural inclinations, nor does it spend itself only upon those for whom some affinity is discovered. Agape love seeks the welfare of all (Rom. 15:2) and works no ill to any (Rom. 13:9–10); love seeks opportunity to do good to "all men, especially unto them who are of the household of faith" (Gal. 6:10).[1]

5. The exercise of charity. Abraham Lincoln marked the following words in one of his favorite books: "The motive power in man is Affection. What he loves, he wills, and what he wills, he performs. Our Character is the complex of all that we love. . . . There is no station in life where there is not a constant demand for the exercise of Charity. We cannot be in company an hour with any person without some such demand presenting itself to us."[2]

6. Putting love into action. A final word of counsel from C. S. Lewis: "Do not waste your time bothering whether you 'love' your neighbor; act as if you did. As soon as we do this, we find one of the great secrets. When you are behaving as if you loved someone, you will presently come to love him. If you injure someone you dislike, you will find yourself disliking him more. If you do him a good turn, you will find yourself disliking him less."[3] Now ask yourself some questions:

‣ Whom has the Lord brought to my mind as I have read these lines?

‣ What specific act might I do to communicate at least something less than hatred or cool contempt or apathy to that person?

‣ What do I think that person's response might be?

‣ What would the response of the Lord be?

▶ What do I have to lose?

7. These people love their pastor! A Methodist family called the Baptist minister to visit a member of the family who was very ill. The Baptist minister knew the family well and was very willing to minister in any way he could, assuming the Methodist pastor was not available. Upon leaving, he asked why he had been called on in such a time, and was told by one of the children, "Actually, our pastor is in town, but our mother has contracted something contagious, and we loved our pastor too much to risk his catching it!"

TEACHING THE BIBLE

▶ *Main Idea*: We should love our neighbors, our enemies, and our fellow Christians.
▶ *Suggested Teaching Aim*: To lead adults to identify similarities and differences between love for neighbors, enemies, and fellow Christians.

A TEACHING OUTLINE

People of Love

1. *Love Your Neighbors (Mark 12:28–34)*
2. *Love Your Enemies (Luke 6:27–36)*
3. *Love One Another (John 13:31–35)*

Introduce the Bible Study

Ask: Whom do you love? What do you love? Why do you love? Say, It isn't hard to tell whom and what we love, but sometimes it is difficult to tell why we love someone or something. Today's lesson will help us identify similarities and differences between love for neighbors, enemies, and fellow Christians.

Search for Biblical Truth

Make three large hearts. Write one of the three outline points from "A Teaching Outline" on each heart. (As an outreach activity, make small hearts and write "People of Love" on one side; on the other side include the time and place of the Bible study, and mail them to members and prospects. Make four large posters by using the four statements in "Summary of Bible Truths." Place these on the wall.

Organize members into three groups. (If your members do not work well in groups, you can use the material as points in a lecture.) **IN ADVANCE**, enlist three members to head up three groups. Give them the following instructions so they can make preparation. On the back of each outline point, list the following instructions:

Group 1
▶ Explain the setting of these verses.
▶ Why do you think the scribe asked Jesus this question (Mark 12:28)?

- What Old Testament Scriptures does Jesus quote in Mark 12:29 and Mark 12:30–31?
- Do you think the scribe was sincere in his question?
- Prepare a case study or a role play that illustrates the truth in these verses.

Group 2
- Explain the setting of these verses.
- What three words did Jesus use to describe how enemies treat people?
- Why do you agree or disagree with this statement: "Christian love is doing good for others, regardless of your feelings toward them or their feelings and actions toward you"?
- What are the four illustrations Jesus gave about how we are to respond in Luke 6:29–30?
- Why would you agree or disagree that the Golden Rule calls for three actions: (1) Put yourself in the other person's shoes; (2) ask yourself, "If I were that person, how would I want to be treated?" and (3) take the initiative in treating the person as you would want to be treated if you were in his or her place.
- Develop a case study or a role play that illustrates the truth in these verses.

Group 3
- Explain the setting of these verses.
- Why would you agree or disagree with the following statements that explain why this could be called a "new commandment": (1) Jesus made love the primary Christian quality; (2) He created a new family of faith and love; (3) He provided the motive, mode, and measure of this love by giving Himself for us.
- What is the result of this kind of love?
- Write a case study or role play that illustrates the truth in these verses.
- Allow time for study and then call for reports.

Give the Truth a Personal Focus

Use "Putting love into action" in "Applying the Bible" to give the truth a personal focus. Write the five questions on a large sheet of paper. If you have time, ask the three groups to respond to these questions and share their responses. If not, use them with the whole group.

---

1. *Vine's Expository Dictionary of Biblical Words* (Nashville: Thomas Nelson, 1985), 382.

2. Carl Sandburg, *Abraham Lincoln: The Prairie Years* (New York: Harcourt, Brace & World, 1926), Vol. 2, pp. 281–292.

3. C. S. Lewis, *Mere Christianity* (New York: Macmillan, 1943), 116.

Kingdom Priorities

Background Passage: Luke 12:13–34
Focal Passage: Luke 12:13–21

Some people complain whenever a Sunday school lesson or sermon deals with money; yet we cannot teach the Bible without dealing with this subject. Jesus had a lot to say about money and possessions. Luke's Gospel is filled with such teachings. Luke 12:13–34 is one powerful example.

▶**Study Aim:** *To evaluate personal priorities in light of Jesus' teachings about kingdom priorities.*

STUDYING THE BIBLE

OUTLINE AND SUMMARY

    I.   **Life Is More Than Possessions (Luke 12:13–15)**
        1. A question about an inheritance (12:13–14)
        2. Life versus possessions (12:15)
    II. **Missing Life Through Greed (Luke 12:16–21)**
        1. A rich man's plans (12:16–19)
        2. The tragedy of missing life (12:20–21)
    III. **Missing Life Through Anxiety (Luke 12:22–29)**
    IV. **Finding Life Through Commitment and Giving (Luke 12:30–34)**

A man asked Jesus to help arbitrate his inheritance, but Jesus refused (12:13–14). Jesus warned against greed and taught that having many possessions does not ensure finding real life (12:15). He told of a rich farmer whose plans for a good harvest showed his greed (12:16–19). The farmer died that night, and God called him a fool (12:20–21). Jesus also warned against missing life through anxiety about food and clothing (12:22–29). Jesus taught that people find life through seeking God's kingdom first and by giving of themselves and their possessions (12:30–34).

I. Life Is More Than Possessions (Luke 12:13–15)

1. A question about an inheritance (12:13–14)

13 And one of the company said unto him, Master, speak to my brother, that he divide the inheritance with me.

14 And he said unto him, Man, who made me a judge or a divider over you?

While Jesus was teaching "an innumerable multitude of people" (Luke 12:1), a man in the crowd spoke to Jesus about helping him get his rightful share of an inheritance. This man was probably a younger brother who felt that his brother had not distributed to him his rightful share of the estate. The Old Testament had laws about inheritances (Num. 27:1–11; 36:7–9; Deut. 21:15–17).

The word translated "Master" is literally "teacher." He hoped that Jesus would intervene on his behalf and use His position as a respected teacher to influence the brother to divide the estate in the right way, perhaps by offering to arbitrate the matter.

Jesus refused to do what the man asked. Jesus' refusal does not mean that the issue was unimportant, nor does it mean that the petitioner did not have a legitimate grievance. Jesus refused because He had no legal standing to handle such legal matters and because He felt this was not what He had come to do.

2. Life versus possessions (12:15)

15 And he said unto them, Take heed, and beware of covetousness: for a man's life consisteth not in the abundance of the things which he possesseth.

Although Jesus refused to get involved in this family dispute, he did use the man's request as an opportunity for instruction. He directed His words not just to the man but also to the entire group (notice the word "them").

Luke 12:15 is one of the most important of Jesus' teachings. The verse contains two parts: a warning and a principle for living. Jesus warned against "covetousness." This word literally means "the desire for more." "Greed" is another word to communicate the idea of desiring more and more. "Covetousness" and "greed" are sometimes used to mean the same thing; however, "covetousness" usually implies greed directed to something that someone else has. The Hebrew word used in the tenth commandment means "desire," but the commandment forbids desiring what belongs to someone else (Exod. 20:17). The man in verse 13 was not so much desiring what belonged to someone else as asking to get what was rightfully his. The rich farmer in Jesus' story (12:16–21) was not coveting what belonged to someone else; he just wanted more and more for himself.

Thus, greed is the insatiable desire to accumulate more and more for oneself. Jesus listed greed (translated "covetousness") as one of the evils that comes from within a sinful heart (Mark 7:22). Paul included covetousness in his lists of sins that ought not to be part of the new life in Christ (Rom. 1:29; Eph. 5:3; Col. 3:5).

The last part of verse 15 is a crucial principle for living. Jesus denied that having many possessions is what life is all about. Life does not consist in the abundance of a person's possessions. People in our society believe just the opposite. They believe that accumulating possessions is the purpose of life because having money and possessions is necessary to pay for the good times and good things of life.

What is the good life? Most people assume it is having enough money to buy what they need and what they want. Jesus said the good life is something different. Having possessions does not guarantee finding life. Many very rich people have missed life; and many poor people have found it (for example, contrast the rich man and Lazarus in Luke 16:19–31).

II. Missing Life Through Greed (Luke 12:16–21)

1. A rich man's plans (12:16–19)

16 And he spake a parable unto them, saying, The ground of a certain rich man brought forth plentifully:

17 And he thought within himself, saying, What shall I do, because I have no room where to bestow my fruits?

18 And he said, This will I do: I will pull down my barns, and build greater; and there will I bestow all my fruits and my goods.

19 And I will say to my soul, Soul, thou hast much goods laid up for many years: take thine ease, eat, drink, and be merry.

Jesus told this story to illustrate His point in verse 15. He told of a rich man, who is typical of many people in every generation. The fact that he was a "rich man" shows that the man already had enough to take care of his needs and those of his family, plus enough to share with others. However, like many people, he wanted to become richer.

Jesus illustrated his desire to become richer by telling of the plans that the man made after he had harvested a bountiful crop. His barns were not large enough to store this rich harvest. Therefore, the obvious solution seemed to be to tear down the old barns and to build new and larger ones.

The farmer's short-range plan was to build the new barns and to place the rich harvest in them. His long-range plan was to retire with the financial security of full barns. This assumption of financial security is seen in his words about "much goods laid up for many years." Then he could begin to live the good life. His dream of this future good life is described by these words, which he promised himself: "Take thine ease, eat, drink, and be merry." "Take thine ease" implies that he had worked hard for many years and was looking forward to retiring from the hard life of a farmer. The other words show that he intended to spend his money or barter his goods to provide plenty to eat and drink and to enjoy life. The word translated "be merry" means to be glad, to rejoice, or to enjoy oneself.

We often think of this meaning a life of sensual self-indulgence; and that may have been what the man meant. The same word, however, was used by the father of the prodigal to describe the family feast to welcome home the wayward son (Luke 15:32). "Having a good time" means different things to different people. All we can say for sure is that the farmer believed that if he had enough possessions, he could retire and really begin to enjoy life.

On the surface, the man seemed to be a sterling example of what many would call "the American dream." He had worked hard, planned well, and become rich. The story contains no hint that he had gained his wealth by dishonest methods or by exploiting others. On the other hand, this honest, hard-working farmer made no mention of either God or others. He spoke only of himself. Notice how often he used the words "I" or "my."

Before the Israelites entered the promised land, Moses warned them of the perils of prosperity. He warned them that after they prospered in

Canaan, they would be tempted to forget the Lord and take credit for their good fortune. The rich farmer was the kind of person that Moses warned would say, "My power and the might of mine hand hath gotten me this wealth" (Deut. 8:17).

The man not only had no time for God; he also showed no evidence of concern for others. He was the opposite kind of person from Barnabas, who had a field that he sold in order to give the money for the needs of the poor (Acts 4:36–37). One purpose of Christian work is to have resources with which to help the needy (Eph. 4:28); however, when this man had a bountiful harvest, he said nothing about sharing any of it.

2. The tragedy of missing life (12:20–21)

20 But God said unto him, Thou fool, this night thy soul shall be required of thee: then whose shall those things be, which thou hast provided?

21 So is he that layeth up treasure for himself, and is not rich toward God.

Keep in mind that all the planning described in verses 16–19 took place in one night. Apparently, on that same night, he died. Nothing is said about the man ever taking time to pray to God, but on that night God spoke to him. He and most of those who knew him thought he was a success, but God called him a fool. Why did God consider the rich man to be a fool?

1. The man failed to recognize the shortness and uncertainty of earthly life. He had not expected to die that night; therefore, he was totally unprepared to face eternity. Like the presumptuous businessmen of James 4:13–16, he acted as if he expected to live forever. James reminded them that life is like "a vapour, that appeareth for a little time, and then vanisheth away" (James 4:14).

2. The man failed to recognize that humans are only trustees of what we call our own. He spoke of his possessions as if he held permanent control over them. God asked him whose these things would belong to after he died. God wasn't dealing with the issue of who would inherit the fruits of his life of hard work. God was simply reminding him that whoever it was, it would not be the man himself.

3. The man missed the point of life itself; and as a result, he missed life. Life involves a right relationship with God and other people. This man spent his days so preoccupied with accumulating possessions that he felt he had no time for God or other people. Jesus painted no picture of this man's fate beyond death. In the later parable of the rich man and Lazarus, the rich man went to hell and Lazarus went to paradise (Luke 16:19–31). The absence of any mention of God or others in the life of the rich farmer of Luke 12:16–19 plus God's judgment of him as a fool strongly implies that these two rich men shared the same eternal destiny.

III. Missing Life Through Anxiety (Luke 12:22–29)

"Take no thought" does not mean not to plan; it translates words meaning "don't be anxious" (12:22, 25, 26). Jesus warned against missing life through greed in Luke 12:16–21; he warned of missing life through anxiety in Luke 12:22–29. He showed that anxiety is a lack of faith. He used God's care of the ravens and the lilies to emphasize that God can be trusted to make available food and clothes for people (12:22, 24, 27–28). Verse 23 echoes the theme of verse 15: Life is more than what we eat and what we wear. Verse 25 shows how futile worry is.

IV. Finding Life Through Commitment and Giving (Luke 12:30–34)

Jesus listed two ways in which people find life: (1) Pagans seek material things; but people of God seek first the kingdom of God, trusting God to provide what they need (12:30–31). (2) Jesus assured His followers of God's love and challenged them to lay up lasting treasures by sharing themselves and their possessions (12:32–33).

SUMMARY OF BIBLE TRUTHS

1. The world equates the good life with having many possessions.
2. Greedy people never have enough; they always want more and more for themselves.
3. Some people are so preoccupied with their possessions that they miss life.
4. Some people live self-centered lives and do not take time for worshiping God or helping others.
5. Tragically, some people ignore the uncertainty of life and die before they truly discover life.

APPLYING THE BIBLE

1. Jesus on money. Consider this statement: "The Lord gave thirty-eight parables in the gospels. Out of those thirty-eight, sixteen are in regard to how we handle our money. Christ said more about money and possessions than about heaven and hell combined. In the gospels, one out of every ten verses deals with money or possessions—288 verses in the four gospels." Why, in your opinion, did our Lord see money management as so important for our lives?

2. The most violated commandment. Billy Graham says that not only have we broken some of the Ten Commandments, but all of us have broken all of them! And he adds another interesting insight: In his view, the tenth—"Thou shalt not covet"—is the most violated of the ten.

3. The tenth commandment today. A university professor of ethics once challenged his class to rearrange the Ten Commandments for the modern world. The only pattern that emerged in the transformation was that many students reversed the first and last. They said that covetousness was the most important commandment in today's world, and putting the Lord God first in all things was the least important. But can we get the covetousness matter right if the worship matter is wrong? Why?

4. Two important words. The words *trustee* and *stewardship* emphasize responsibility and accountability in regards to the use of money. A trustee holds something else "in trust" for another (to whom he must give an account). The English word *stewardship* originally meant a "warden of the sty"—the keeper or manager of a pig pen—(and so, again, he had to give an account to the owner.)

5. God's Little Acre. Erskine Caldwell wrote a popular novel, *God's Little Acre,* in 1933. It was the story of poor Southern mountaineers, shiftless ne'er-do-wells, who had a very shallow view of life and of God. The title of the book came from the custom, somewhat widespread in the rural South in times gone by, of setting aside an acre, the produce of which belonged to the Lord. The head of the clan constantly shifted the acre's location according to his own financial whims, and the Lord never seemed to get His promised portion. Discuss how we moderns continue to play that same game with the Lord.

6. The Lord's calf. A cow gave birth to twins, and the farmer told his wife he would give one of the calves to the Lord. Time went by and, no matter how his wife insisted, the farmer would never say which calf belonged to the Lord and which belonged to him. One day he came in after chores and said, "Molly, guess what? The Lord's calf done gone and died!"

7. Dangerous information. According to one story, a man died and his will revealed that he had left $100,000 to his ailing father. His sister asked the pastor, in view of her father's failing health, to bring the news of the inheritance gently to her father. The pastor asked, "Brother Jones, if the Lord gave you $100,000, what would you do with it?" The man replied, "Well, of course, I'd give it to the church." The pastor suffered a heart attack! I heard of another man who said he didn't want all the land on earth, only that which touched his. And another man who said he always decided what to give the Lord by "throwing all the money he had every Sunday morning up into the air and letting the Lord keep all that didn't come down."

TEACHING THE BIBLE

▶ *Main Idea:* Christians' personal priorities are shaped by Jesus' teachings about kingdom priorities.

▶ *Suggested Teaching Aim:* To lead adults to evaluate personal priorities in light of Jesus' teachings about kingdom priorities.

A TEACHING OUTLINE

Kingdom Priorities

1. *Life Is More Than Possessions (Luke 12:13–15)*
2. *Missing Life Through Greed (Luke 12:16–21)*
3. *Missing Life Through Anxiety (Luke 12:22–29)*
4. *Finding Life Through Commitment and Giving (Luke 30–34)*

Introduce the Bible Study

Read this case study: Bill had grown up in the inner city. Through a lot of hard work and the encouragement of a teacher, he graduated from high school, received a college scholarship, and graduated at the top of his class. He went on to graduate school and got his masters degree in business administration. He landed a job with one of the Fortune 500 companies and by the time he was forty, he was a millionaire. Ask: What's wrong with this picture? How does it differ from the one Jesus told about the rich farmer?

Search for Biblical Truth

IN ADVANCE, copy "A Teaching Outline" on four strips.

Copy the four summary statements from "Outline and Summary" on one color of paper and the Scripture references on a sheet of another color. Place both of these at random around the room. Ask members to match the statement with the appropriate Scripture. Read the Suggested Teaching Aim.

Place the first outline strip on the wall and ask a volunteer to read Luke 12:13–15. Use a brief lecture to summarize the material in "Studying the Bible."

DISCUSS: For a Christian, what constitutes the good life? Can a person have money and be a committed follower of Jesus? Explain your answer.

Place the second outline strip on the wall and ask a volunteer to read Luke 12:16–21. Use a brief lecture to summarize the material in "Studying the Bible."

DISCUSS: How does this rich farmer differ from the man in the case study at the beginning of the lesson? What are some warning signs that we may be in danger of becoming like them? Do we have to have a lot of money to have this attitude?

Using the material in "Studying the Bible," explain why God considered the man to be a fool:

(1) The man failed to recognize the shortness and uncertainty of earthly life.

(2) The man failed to recognize that humans are only trustees of what we call our own.

(3) The man missed the point of life itself; and as a result, he missed life.

Place the last two outline points on the wall, and since they do not have any focal passage Scripture in them, summarize the material briefly.

Read the five statements in "Summary of Bible Truths."

Give the Truth a Personal Focus

IN ADVANCE, make a poster with these words: "This night thy soul shall be required of thee." Place the poster on the wall. Ask members to close their eyes and bow their heads. Ask: If God spoke these words to you today, would you be satisfied to enter eternity with your current attitude toward possessions? What are you satisfied with? What would need changing? How much eternal good have you done with your material possessions? How have you helped the kingdom? Provide a moment of silent reflection to allow members time to answer these questions for themselves.

Reversing the World's Standard

Background Passages: Matthew 18:1–4; 20:17–28
Focal Passages: Matthew 18:1–4; 20:17–28

Who is the greatest person in your community? in your church? How a person answers these questions shows the person's standards for defining greatness. The world defines greatness in terms of power, wealth, and fame. Jesus reversed those standards by defining greatness in terms of self-giving service.

▶**Study Aim:** *To distinguish the world's standard from Jesus' standard of greatness.*

STUDYING THE BIBLE

OUTLINE AND SUMMARY
  I. **Who Is the Greatest? (Matt. 18:1–4)**
      1. **The disciples' question (18:1)**
      2. **Jesus' response (18:2–4)**
  II. **Greatness Is Self-giving Service (Matt. 20:17–28)**
      1. **Third prediction of Jesus' death (20:17–19)**
      2. **Request for places of honor (20:20–21)**
      3. **Jesus' response to the request (20:22–23)**
      4. **Anger of the other disciples (20:24)**
      5. **Two contrasting standards (20:25–27)**
      6. **The Suffering Servant (20:28)**

The disciples asked Jesus who is greatest in the kingdom of heaven (18:1). Jesus used a child to show that childlikeness is essential to enter and to be great in God's kingdom (18:2–4). Jesus predicted His death for the third time (20:17–19). James, John, and their mother asked for the two brothers to have places of honor in the kingdom (20:20–21). Jesus said that such places were not His to give and that following Him would mean suffering (20:22–23). The other ten disciples were outraged at the brothers' request (20:24). Jesus reminded them that the standard for greatness in the world is power and authority, but that His standard is self-giving service (20:25–27). Jesus Himself did not come to be served but to serve and to give His life to redeem sinners (20:28).

I. Who Is the Greatest? (Matt. 18:1–4)

1. The disciples' question (18:1)

1 At the same time came the disciples unto Jesus, saying, Who is the greatest in the kingdom of heaven?

The disciples had discussed this question privately. When they did, they were arguing about which of them was the greatest (Mark 9:33–34; Luke 9:46). This personal and private argument was probably the basis for the more general question in Matthew 18:1. They asked Jesus to say who is the greatest in the kingdom. They seemed to have in mind a kingdom with earthly standards of greatness based on power, prestige, and position.

2. Jesus' response (18:2–4)

2 And Jesus called a little child unto him, and set him in the midst of them,

3 And said, Verily I say unto you, Except ye be converted, and become as little children, ye shall not enter into the kingdom of heaven.

4 Whosoever therefore shall humble himself as this little child, the same is greatest in the kingdom of heaven.

Jesus was sensitive to little children (Matt. 19:13–15; Mark 9:36). On this occasion, Jesus had already taken notice of a child nearby. He called the child, who quickly obeyed. Then Jesus placed the child in the middle of the group and said that becoming as little children is necessary to enter the kingdom.

It was as if Jesus said, "Here is the greatest in the kingdom." If He had said that, the disciples would have been appalled. Little children in that day had no status. They were completely dependent on adults. Not only did children have no status or claim to greatness, they claimed none. They accepted their lack of importance. They thus were good examples of the first beatitude, "Blessed are the poor in spirit; for theirs is the kingdom of heaven" (Matt. 5:3). The first quality of kingdom citizens is accepting our poverty of spirit. This is another way of saying, accepting our complete dependence on God and His grace.

As soon as Jesus called, this child came to Him. Little children are quicker to hear the Savior's call and obey Him. Adults are often slow to respond for fear of what others will say. In order to enter the kingdom, people must turn from their sins (including selfish ambition like that of the disciples) and become dependent and responsive as little children.

Verse 4 shows that becoming as little children is not only the entrance qualification to the kingdom but also the measure of greatness in the kingdom. The disciples—whatever their age—who remain humble in attitude toward the Lord and one another are the greatest in the kingdom.

II. Greatness Is Self-Giving Service (Matt. 20:17–28)

1. Third prediction of Jesus' death (20:17–19)

17 And Jesus going up to Jerusalem took the twelve disciples apart in the way, and said unto them,

18 Behold, we go up to Jerusalem; and the Son of man shall be betrayed unto the chief priests and unto the scribes, and they shall condemn him to death,

19 And shall deliver him to the Gentiles to mock, and to scourge, and to crucify him: and the third day he shall rise again.

Right after Peter's confession, Jesus had first predicted His coming death and resurrection (Matt. 16:21). The second prediction came after the transfiguration (Matt. 17:22–23). Now as they approached Jerusalem, Jesus took the disciples aside and added details to His earlier predictions. He revealed that the Jewish religious leaders would condemn Jesus and send Him to the Gentiles. Jesus also predicted that the Gentiles would mock, scourge, and crucify Him.

The disciples' responses to these predictions show that they still did not understand why Jesus kept making this strange prediction (Mark 9:32). Their actions show how much they missed His point. At the last supper, the disciples were still arguing about which of them was the greatest (Luke 22:24). And right after the third prediction came the request that two of His disciples be promised the two most important places in the kingdom.

2. Request for places of honor (20:20–21)

20 Then came to him the mother of Zebedee's children with her sons, worshipping him, and desiring a certain thing of him.

21 And he said unto her, What wilt thou? She saith unto him, Grant that these my two sons may sit, the one on thy right hand, and the other on the left, in thy kingdom.

Mark 10:35 reports that James and John came, but it makes no mention of their mother. Matthew shows that she also came and actually made the request; however, the fact that Jesus addressed His response to the brothers shows that they were key players in this drama. (The traditional interpretation of Matthew 27:56 and Mark 15:40 is that Salome was the sister of Jesus' mother and the mother of James and John. If so, she and they may have felt that relatives should have first claim on the two chief places in the kingdom.)

3. Jesus' response to the request (20:22–23)

22 But Jesus answered and said, Ye know not what ye ask. Are ye able to drink of the cup that I shall drink of, and to be baptized with the baptism that I am baptized with? They say unto him, We are able.

23 And he saith unto them, Ye shall drink indeed of my cup, and be baptized with the baptism that I am baptized with: but to sit on my right hand, and on my left, is not mine to give, but it shall be given to them for whom it is prepared of my Father.

James and John thought of these as places of honor and glory, but Jesus knew that to reign with Him also meant suffering with Him (Rom. 8:17). The "cup" in the Old Testament could represent joy (Ps. 23:5) or suffering (Ps. 75:8). Jesus here obviously meant a cup of suffering. This is how He used the term in His Gethsemane prayer (Matt. 26:39). Likewise, baptism meant dying (Luke 12:50). He asked the brothers if they were able to drink of His cup.

Their quick response represented ignorance more than arrogance. Jesus sadly noted that in a sense, they would drink His cup. Although James and John then thought of places of honor, James later was the first of the apostles to be put to death (Acts 12:1–2). John lived to be an old man, but late in life he was exiled to a lonely island (Rev. 1:9). Jesus said that only the Father could determine such things as seats on His right and left hand.

4. Anger of the other disciples (20:24)

24 And when the ten heard it, they were moved with indignation against the two brethren.

The other disciples apparently were not present when James and John made their request, but they soon heard about it. Their predictable response was fiery anger. They were outraged not because of the inappropriateness of such a request but because James and John got their request in first. If anyone should have been righteously indignant, it was Jesus; however, He continued to show remarkable patience with all these status-seeking followers.

5. Two contrasting standards (20:25–27)

25 But Jesus called them unto him, and said, Ye know that the princes of the Gentiles exercise dominion over them, and they that are great exercise authority upon them.

26 But it shall not be so among you: but whosoever will be great among you, let him be your minister;

27 And whosoever will be chief among you, let him be your servant.

The so-called great ones in the nonbelieving world are people who exercise positions of power and authority over other people. The greatest are those who have power and authority over the most people. This standard of greatness in the first-century Greco-Roman world has not changed in twenty centuries. Power and authority mean wealth and fame. These are how the nonbelieving world today still defines greatness.

The word translated "chief" literally means "first." Jesus had just taught how the last will be first, and the first will be last (Matt. 19:30; 20:16). People in the world want to be number one—first. This is another way to define greatness. But Jesus said that those who are first and great in the world's eyes usually are last and least in God's eyes, while the last and least in the world's eyes are often the first and greatest in God's eyes.

The greatest ones in God's kingdom are the servants and the slaves. The word translated "be minister" in verse 26 means to be a servant. The word translated "be servant" in verse 27 means to be a slave. Slaves were at the bottom of the social world, and servants (not actual slaves owned by someone) were a close second. Jesus said that people who serve others in God's name are the great ones in God's eyes.

6. The Suffering Servant (20:28)

28 Even as the Son of man came not to be ministered unto, but to minister, and to give his life a ransom for many.

Philippians 2:6–8 is a good parallel passage. The eternal Son of God gave up the glories of heaven to become a human being, to live a life of service, and to die the most humiliating of deaths. He was born to a poor young woman. His first crib was a manger. His first visitors were humble shepherds. During His life, He gave Himself in acts of sacrificial service for others. Of course, at times He accepted acts of service to Him from those who loved Him (Matt. 8:15; Luke 8:3; John 12:1–8). However,

Jesus came to serve, not to be served like some earthly king. On His last night, He performed the humble task of washing the disciples' feet—something they had been too proud to do (John 13:1–17).

His death for sinners was His ultimate act of self-giving, sacrificial love. He laid down His life to provide a ransom for those enslaved by sin and death. "Many" probably comes from Isaiah 53:10–12, the passage that was fulfilled in the death of the Suffering Servant. Since God's love is not willing that any perish (2 Pet. 3:9), "many" probably represents the fact that not everyone receives Him (see John 3:16; 2 Cor. 5:14; 1 Tim. 2:6; Heb. 2:9, which use words like "world," "whosoever," and "all").

SUMMARY OF BIBLE TRUTHS

1. The world measures greatness by prominence and power.
2. Jesus measures greatness by humble, self-giving service.
3. Jesus Himself is the perfect example of true greatness.
4. Christians are tempted to follow the world's standard.
5. Christians should live by heaven's standard.

APPLYING THE BIBLE

1. Helping others. Sir Bartel Fere was the English governor of Bombay in the last century. He was known far and wide as "the helping man." A new servant was sent to meet him upon his arrival home after a long trip. The servant asked, "How will I recognize him?" Fere's wife said, "Look for a tall gentleman helping somebody, and you'll have your man." If a half dozen of your best friends were to identify your most distinguishing characteristic, what would it be? Or, if your pastor, at your funeral service, stated the three most marked traits of your personality, what would they be?

2. We must love specific people. The Russian novelist Dostoyevsky once wrote, "I love humanity, but I wonder at myself. The more I love humanity in general, the less I love man in particular. In my dreams I have often come to making enthusiastic schemes for the service of humanity and perhaps I might actually have faced crucifixion if it had been suddenly necessary; and yet I am incapable of living in the same room with anyone for two days together."[1]

3. Sharing with others. When I first came to Christ, I heard an unforgettable story about service. It seems that a situation occurred in hell in which everybody had very long arms. There was plenty of food, but the people's arms were so long they could not feed themselves. It seems the same long-armed condition existed in heaven, but everyone ate in heaven because the people there fed each other! The point is this: Pride caused sadness in hell, and love caused joy in heaven.

4. Helping others helps you. "As (Hans) Selye explained it, and as I learned more about it from his landmark book, *The Stress of Life,* altruistic egoism is nothing more than the biblical truth that helping others helps you. Selye had learned that those who earn the goodwill of their neighbors are dramatically better off psychologically and physiologically than those who are looked upon as selfish and greedy."[2]

5. Selfless service.

"People can be unreasonable, illogical, and self-centered;
LOVE THEM ANYWAY.
If you do good, some will accuse you of selfish motives;
DO GOOD ANYWAY.
If you succeed, you may win false friends and true enemies;
SUCCEED ANYWAY.
The good you do today may be forgotten tomorrow;
DO GOOD ANYWAY.
Honesty and frankness make you vulnerable;
BE HONEST ANYWAY.
What takes years to build may be destroyed overnight;
BUILD WELL ANYWAY."

6. Serve Christ by serving others. Matthew 25:31–40 records perhaps the truth most difficult for us to conceive: that in serving others, we serve Christ Himself. A profound change in our service to others would result from remembering that! Jesus, in the "cup of cold water" passage (Matt. 10:40–42), said the same thing. In Edwin Markham's poem, "How the Great Guest Came," our Lord says to one who has, unknowingly, served Him by serving others:

> Three times I came by your friendly door;
> Three times my shadow was on your floor.
> I was the beggar with bruised feet;
> I was the woman you gave to eat;
> I was the child on the homeless street.[3]

7. For discussion. Is it not interesting that when we use the word *successful* about others, it invariably assumes wealth? Who are the people who come to mind, in your church or community, who are known not for their wealth but for their service? Would you classify them as successful? Would others say that about you? What makes it so difficult to serve others?

TEACHING THE BIBLE

▶ *Main Idea:* The world's standard of greatness differs from Jesus' standard for His disciples.

▶ *Suggested Teaching Aim:* To lead adults to distinguish Jesus' standard of greatness from the world's standard of greatness.

A TEACHING OUTLINE

Reversing the World's Standard

1. *Who Is the Greatest? (Matt. 18:1–4)*
2. *Jesus Illustrates Self-giving Service (Matt. 20:17–19)*
3. *The Disciples Illustrate Selfish Service (Matt. 20:20–24)*
4. *The Two Standards Contrasted (Matt. 20:25–28)*

Introduce the Bible Study

Use the illustration of "Helping others" in "Applying the Bible" to introduce the lesson. Ask members to think of their response to this question: Based upon your life up to this point, how would people identify you?

Search for Biblical Truth

IN ADVANCE, write the four points in "A Teaching Outline" on a poster and display it on the focal wall. Cover points 2–4 until you are ready to teach them.

Point to outline point 1. Ask members to open their Bibles to Matthew 18 and read verses 1–4. Ask: Why do you think the disciples asked this question? What kind of a kingdom did they apparently visualize? Why do you think Jesus answered by giving an object lesson with a child? What lessons did Jesus teach by His actions?

Uncover the second outline point. Ask members to scan Matthew 20:17–19. Using the material in "Studying the Bible," lecture briefly, pointing out (1) the two earlier references Jesus had made about death; (2) the disciples' response showed they had missed Jesus' point about greatness.

Ask members to scan Matthew 20:20–24. Explain (1) Salome's request for her sons came immediately after Jesus' announcement about His death; (2) she had misinterpreted Jesus' kingdom as well; (3) the meaning of "cup" and "baptism" in this context; (4) what happened to James and John that showed they did drink the cup and participated in Jesus' baptism; (5) even so, only the Father could grant special seating in the kingdom of heaven; (6) the other disciples were angry because they hadn't gotten their request in to Jesus before James and John.

DISCUSS: Why do you think Matthew mentions the mother of James and John making this request and Mark's Gospel (10:35) does not mention her?

Uncover the fourth outline point. Ask members to search Matthew 20:25–28 and identify the two contrasting standards of the world and of Jesus. On a chalkboard or a large sheet of paper write **World's Standards** in one column and **Jesus' Standards** in another. Ask members to list characteristics of both of these.

Read the five statements in "Summary of Bible Truths" one at a time; ask members why they agree or disagree with each statement.

Give the Truth a Personal Focus

Ask: Based upon your actions this past week, which of the two standards do you fulfill? Distribute paper and pencils. Ask members to write three steps they can take to change their actions to reflect Jesus' standard. Ask them to choose one of these steps and to write a specific plan for accomplishing it or at least starting it this coming week.

---

1. William Dyal Jr., *It's Worth Your Life* (New York: Association Press, 1967), 134.
2. Quoted in Bob Buford, *Halftime: Changing Your Game Plan from Success to Significance* (Grand Rapids: Zondervan, 1994), 141.
3. *Bartlett's Familiar Quotations,* 13th ed. (Boston: Little, Brown, 1955), 756.

Forgiving Each Other

Background Passage: Matthew 18:6–35
Focal Passage: Matthew 18:21–35

Forgiving others is an important expression of Christian love. Jesus taught that God forgives us our sins out of His great love and that those who have experienced His forgiveness should be forgiving toward others.

▶**Study Aim:** *To explain why being forgiven by God and forgiving others are inseparable.*

STUDYING THE BIBLE

OUTLINE AND SUMMARY

   I. **Concern for Little Ones (Matt. 18:6–14)**
      1. **Beware causing a little one to stumble (18:6–9)**
      2. **Share the Father's love for little ones (18:10–14)**
  II. **Forgiving Your Brother (Matt. 18:15–22)**
      1. **Seeking reconciliation (18:15–20)**
      2. **How often forgive? (18:21–22)**
 III. **Forgive as God Forgives (Matt. 18:23–35)**
      1. **Forgiving an unpayable debt (18:23–27)**
      2. **Refusing to forgive a smaller debt (18:28–30)**
      3. **The unforgiving are unforgivable (18:31–35)**

God will punish those who cause little ones to stumble (18:6–9). He is not willing that one little one perish (18:10–14). If someone sins against you, do everything possible to be reconciled (18:15–20). Jesus taught unlimited forgiveness (18:21–22). A king forgave a servant a huge, unpayable debt (18:23–27). The forgiven servant refused to forgive a smaller debt (18:28–30). Being unforgiving makes one unforgivable (18:31–35).

I. Concern for Little Ones (Matt. 18:6–14)

1. Beware causing a little one to stumble (18:6–9)

"Little ones" are children or those who enter the kingdom like little children (Matt. 18:1–4). Special care needs to be given to avoid causing one to stumble (18:6–7). Radical surgery of an offending part of one's body is preferable to falling into sin or leading someone else astray (18:8–9).

2. Share the Father's love for little ones (18:10–14)

The Father has special love for little ones (18:10). The Son of man came to seek and to save the lost (18:11). Just as a good shepherd seeks a lost sheep, so does God seek the straying (18:12–13). He is not willing that one little one perish (18:14).

II. Forgiving Your Brother (Matt. 18:15–22)

1. Seeking reconciliation (18:15–20)

If your brother has sinned against you, you should go privately and seek reconciliation (18:15; compare Matt. 5:23). If your brother is unwilling, take two or three others and renew the effort (18:16). If the brother is still unrepentant, take the problem to the church; and if he refuses to hear the church, consider the person an outsider (18:17). Matthew 18:18–19 does not refer to ecclesiastical authority to forgive sins, but to the responsibility of believers to offer forgiveness in Christ's name (18:18–19). Christ is present wherever two or three meet in His name (18:20).

2. How often forgive? (18:21–22)

21 Then came Peter to him, and said, LORD, How oft shall my brother sin against me, and I forgive him? till seven times?

22 Jesus saith unto him, I say not unto thee, Until seven times: but, Until seventy times seven.

Peter had heard what Jesus said about seeking reconciliation with a brother who sinned against him (18:15). Peter wondered, How many times am I supposed to forgive? This was not just an academic question because forgiveness is not easy. The rabbis taught that one should forgive up to three times, but no more. They based that on Amos 1:3, 6, 9, 11, 13; 2:1, 4, 6. Peter knew that Jesus usually went beyond legal requirements, so he asked if seven times was enough.

Jesus said that seven was not enough, but seventy times seven. He was not saying to forgive 490 times but not 491 times. His point was not to keep count because forgiveness is unlimited. How many times does God forgive us—sometimes even for the same sin?

III. Forgive as God Forgives (Matt. 18:23–35)

1. Forgiving an unpayable debt (18:23–27)

23 Therefore is the kingdom of heaven likened unto a certain king, which would take account of his servants.

24 And when he had begun to reckon, one was brought unto him, which owed him ten thousand talents.

25 But forasmuch as he had not to pay, his lord commanded him to be sold, and his wife, and children, and all that he had, and payment to be made.

26 The servant therefore fell down, and worshipped him, saying, Lord, have patience with me, and I will pay thee all.

27 Then the lord of that servant was moved with compassion, and loosed him, and forgave him the debt.

The parable of the unforgiving servant is one of the longest of Jesus' parables. Like most of His parables, not everything in the story was intended to be a part of the lesson. Nor was everything realistic to how real life is. Jesus used exaggeration.

Jesus told of a pagan king who called his servants in to give account of how well they were serving him. One servant owed the king ten thousand talents. This is difficult to define in current dollars, but it was an enormous amount. A talent was the highest denomination of money then known, and ten thousand was the highest number for which the Greek language had words. No servant would ever have been able to accumulate such a debt.

The king's order to sell his family and put him into prison was realistic enough for pagan kings. Jewish kings were forbidden to do this, but pagan creditors often sold a family to recover part of the debt. Faced with such a prospect, the debtor pleaded for patience and promised to pay the entire debt. No servant could ever pay back ten thousand talents.

The king's compassion was not typical of pagan kings, but it is true of God the King to whom we sinners owe a debt that we can never pay. "Moved with compassion" is the same word used of Jesus in Matthew 9:36 and Luke 7:13, and of the father of the prodigal in Luke 15:20. Verse 27 says that the king released the man and forgave his debt. The word *forgave* is the same word used to express forgiveness of sin. It means to remove sin as a barrier between the forgiving person or God and the sinner who repents.

Debt is only one of the words used in the Bible to describe sin. It communicates what we owe God and have failed to give Him. However, debt is too impersonal to communicate the terrible hurt inflicted by sin. We get that in stories of personal hurts—like the father of the prodigal or the hurt that the prophet Hosea felt when his wife was unfaithful. God feels the pain and betrayal caused by our sins (Hos. 11:1–4). Forgiveness exacts a cost from the person who forgives. The forgiving person must absorb the hurt of the sin in order to set it aside. That is what God did at the cross.

2. Refusing to forgive a smaller debt (18:28–30)

28 But the same servant went out, and found one of his fellowservants, which owed him an hundred pence: and he laid hands on him, and took him by the throat, saying, Pay me that thou owest.

29 And his fellowservant fell down at his feet, and besought him, saying, Have patience with me, and I will pay thee all.

30 And he would not: but went and cast him into prison, till he should pay the debt.

The newly forgiven servant was creditor to another servant. A "penny" (plural "pence" in 18:28) in Matthew 20:2 translated the word *denarius*. This was the amount a laborer received for a day's work. The amount a laborer would receive for working one hundred days was no small amount to a laborer, but it was a drop in the bucket compared to ten thousand talents. With diligence and hard work, this debt could be paid. The debtor promised to do just that. In fact, both debtors used the same plea, "Have patience with me, and I will pay thee all" (18:26, 29). However, the newly forgiven servant was unwilling to forgive a fellowservant who owed a much smaller amount. He refused and had the man thrown into prison.

The obvious point in verses 28–30 is the inconsistency of the man who had been forgiven the unpayable debt. One would expect him to have learned how terrible it is to face the prospect of prison and how wonderful to be forgiven. Yet this man seemed not to have learned anything from his experience.

A secondary lesson may be in the amount of the debt he was owed. Jesus could have made it much smaller: an amount equal to only a few days' wages; however, He made it one hundred days' wages. This perhaps was intended to remind us how hard it is to forgive someone. Real forgiveness is called for in human relations when a person has been deeply hurt by someone else. Galatians 6:1 calls for Christians to seek to restore fellow believers who have sinned. It is one thing to do this for sin in general; it is something else to do it if the sin has deeply injured you personally.

Forgiveness is not the same as forbearance. Forbearance is putting up with the petty annoyances of relating to another person. Forgiveness is absorbing the pain of being deeply hurt. This is not easy to do. As in God's case, forgiving someone exacts a price. You must absorb the hurt without retaliating. You must set it aside as a barrier to future relations. You must be reconciled to the other person.

3. The unforgiving are unforgivable (18:31–35)

31 So when his fellowservants saw what was done, they were very sorry, and came and told unto their lord all that was done.

32 Then his lord, after that he had called him, said unto him, O thou wicked servant, I forgave thee all that debt, because thou desirest me:

33 Shouldest not thou also have had compassion on thy fellowservant, even as I had pity on thee?

34 And his lord was wroth, and delivered him to the tormentors, till he should pay all that was due unto him.

35 So likewise shall my heavenly Father do also unto you, if ye from your hearts forgive not every one his brother their trespasses.

The other servants, deeply grieved by the unforgiving servant, made a full report to the king. The king, furious at this injustice, called in the "wicked servant." He rebuked him for failing to show the same kind of compassion that the king had shown him. The king then reinstated the debt and turned the unforgiving servant over to the torturers until he paid all he owned.

Verse 35 states the point of the parable. Yet even here we must be careful about how we explain what Jesus taught about the relationship between God's forgiveness of our sins and our forgiveness of those who hurt us. His main point is that they are inseparable. Being forgiven by God ought to result in showing forgiveness toward others. An unforgiving person is unforgivable. This is a consistent teaching of Jesus. He taught us to pray, "Forgive us our debts, as we forgive our debtors" (Matt. 6:12). Matthew 6:14–15 amplifies this prayer.

Jesus did not mean that forgiving others is a good work that merits divine forgiveness. Jesus meant that forgiveness is like a two-way street, not a one-way street. The traffic must move in both directions, not just one. If your heart is open to receive God's forgiveness, your heart is open to let your forgiveness flow out. If your heart is closed in either direction, it is closed in both directions.

Jesus did not mean that God takes back His forgiveness from Christians who commit the sin of not forgiving others. Jesus did mean that an unforgiving spirit is a serious sin. It either shows that someone has never really experienced divine forgiveness or that a forgiven person is committing a serious sin against the Lord as well as against the person who needs that person's forgiveness.

What part does repentance play in this dynamic? Luke 17:3–4 assumes that the one who hurt you asks you for forgiveness. In the parable of the unforgiving servant, both servants asked for mercy. Matthew 18:15–20 assumes that repentance as well as forgiveness are necessary for reconciliation. Of course, if someone hurts you and refuses to repent, you should still display a spirit that is eager for reconciliation.

SUMMARY OF BIBLE TRUTHS

1. Sin is like a huge debt to God that we can never pay.
2. God in love forgives us this debt when we repent.
3. Forgiveness is costly for the person forgiving.
4. Those whom God has forgiven should forgive others.
5. An unforgiving spirit is a serious sin.

APPLYING THE BIBLE

1. Forgiveness. *In this lesson* we study one of the truly "hard sayings" of our Lord. What is it? It is this: Unless we forgive others, we have no right to expect Him to forgive us! Many have attempted to soften His word and make it something less than He intended. But listen to how C. S. Lewis puts it: "To forgive the incessant provocations of daily life—to keep on forgiving the bossy mother-in-law, the bullying husband, the nagging wife, the selfish daughter, the deceitful son—how can we do it? Only, I think, by remembering where we stand, by meaning our words when we say in our prayers each night 'Forgive us our trespasses as we forgive those that trespass against us.' We are offered forgiveness on no other terms. To refuse it is to refuse God's mercy for ourselves. There is no hint of exceptions and God means what he says."[1] But doesn't that sound like "legalism" and contrary to grace? Surely the safest way to look at it is not to ask whether it is law or grace, but to obey God about it. Obedience always wins the day over understanding!

2. Freedom from hatred. R. G. Lee wrote, "A man who is master of himself is not free to do his best work, until he can stand on his feet and say: 'There is not a soul on earth against whom I could lift my finger with a desire to hurt him, nor is there a single human being whom I have either the time or disposition to hate.' Of course, somebody has injured you. Your misfortune would be honeycomb to somebody. But a sense of injury is aggravated by remembrance and a grudge is the heaviest load you ever carried."[2]

3. Try this checklist for forgiveness. Those of us who have a difficult time forgiving focus on seven responses: (1) Focus on God. After all, forgiveness is for His sake first. "Forgive . . . forget . . . for God!" Far too much emphasis is made on the effect of unforgiveness on humans and not on the plain command of God. (2) Focus on yourself. What harm is unforgiveness doing to you? (3) Focus on those close to you. What is your unforgiving spirit doing to your loved ones? (4) Focus on the one who wronged you. Give him or her the benefit of the doubt, remembering, "All things you would that men should do unto you, do ye even so to them." (5) Focus on the Scriptures. See especially Romans 12:9–21, where we are told five times not to retaliate (verses 14, 17, 19, 20, and 21). (6) Focus on the cross. I was praying once about somebody who had wronged me. It was as if I was kneeling before the cross, and I heard the Lord asking me, "How's that again? Before you go any farther, you might move over so My blood won't fall on you." That word from Him changed my prayer dramatically! (7) Focus on your funeral! Will you be glad when the minister says something like this at your funeral. "Here lies a person who never forgave anybody! He's not famous for much, but he's in the *Guinness Book of World Records* for unforgiveness! What a person!"

4. A professional hater. Listen to a paragraph from a letter I received from one of our television viewers some time ago. (I receive the most mail when I preach on bitterness or an unforgiving spirit!) The writer said: "How do you fight hatred? I never learned to hate but my husband is a professional at it—and has involved our grown children." A professional hater! I had never thought of such a thing! Maybe, like football and basketball and baseball and hockey, there is an LPH—a "League of Professional Haters!" Would you make the all-star team? How would you have counseled this woman?

5. God forgives us. "When John Newton died, he had a banner placed across from his bed. On the banner, he had his friends write the words of Psalm 32, 'Blessed is he whose transgression is forgiven, whose sin is covered.' Newton died gazing on those words. He understood."[3]

6. Holding grudges causes us to doubt that others have forgiven us. There was a boy with several nickels who knew a girl who had several marbles. Earnestly desiring to make a deal with her, he said, "I'll give you all my nickels if you'll give me all your marbles." She agreed, and the swap was made—except that, unknown by her, he kept back one of his nickels. His problem: He later said that for many years he wondered—and still does—whether she gave him all her marbles!

7. For discussion and action. Who is it from whom you ought to seek forgiveness? Who is it that you ought to contact and assure that you have completely forgiven them? Who is it that you ought—as a compassionate and caring brother or sister in Christ—to encourage to seek, or give, forgiveness? What grudge is your family or your church holding that is preventing the full blessing of God?

TEACHING THE BIBLE

▶ *Main Idea:* Being forgiven by God ought to result in our showing forgiveness toward others.
▶ *Suggested Teaching Aim:* To lead adults to explain why being forgiven by God and forgiving others are inseparable.

A TEACHING OUTLINE

Forgiving Each Other

1. *Concern for Little Ones (Matt. 18:6–15)*
2. *Forgiving Your Brother (Matt. 18:15–22)*
3. *Forgive as God Forgives (Matt. 18:23–35)*

Introduce the Bible Study

Use the quote from C. S. Lewis in "Forgiveness" in "Applying the Bible." Ask: How do you react to these words? Do they seem a little harsh? Why?

Search for Biblical Truth

IN ADVANCE, make posters with these numbers on them—3, 7, 7x70—and place them around the room. Point to the posters and ask: How often do we forgive someone? Ask members to open their Bibles to Matthew 18:21–22. Explain (1) the rabbis' teaching that one should forgive three times; (2) Peter's question about forgiving seven times; (3) Jesus' statement to forgive seven times seventy. Ask: How many times does God forgive us—sometimes for the same sin?

IN ADVANCE, enlist two people to read aloud Matthew 18:23–27, alternating verses. Use the material in "Studying the Bible" to explain how great a debt the unforgiving servant owed. Ask: Why do you think Jesus used exaggeration to make His point? Ask: How is our sin like or unlike a huge debt? What does it cost someone to forgive?

Read aloud 18:28–30. Explain the debt the fellowservant owed and point out that both debtors used the same plea. Ask: Why do you think the unforgiving servant acted like he did? After members have responded, ask: Why do you think we don't forgive others?

Ask members to look at 18:31–35. On a chalkboard or a large sheet of paper write *King* and *God*. Ask members to describe the king and list characteristics under *King*. Then ask them to compare how our heavenly Father is both alike and different from the king.

Ask members to find a verse that sums up the point of the parable. (v. 35.) On a chalkboard write the words *God* and *Others*. Between the two draw a large arrow pointing both directions. On the arrow write *Us*. Explain that forgiveness is like a two-way street. The traffic must move in both directions, not just one. If our hearts are open to receive God's forgiveness, our heart is open to let forgiveness flow out. If our hearts are closed in either direction, it is closed in both directions.

Ask the two enlisted readers to read the five statements in "Summary of Bible Truths."

Give the Truth a Personal Focus

On a chalkboard draw a picture of a bucket filled with mud. Ask: How much water can a bucket filled with mud hold? How much forgiveness can a life filled with hatred hold?

Use "Holding grudges causes us to doubt that others have forgiven us" from "Applying the Bible." Encourage members to receive God's forgiveness and to forgive others because they have been forgiven.

Point to the number posters. Ask: Which of these comes closest to representing the number of times God has forgiven you? Which comes closest to representing the number of times you have forgiven someone else? Would you claim God's help in bringing the number of times you have forgiven a little closer to the number of times God has forgiven you? Close in prayer that this may happen to all lives.

1. C. S. Lewis, *The Weight of Glory* (New York: Macmillan, 1947), 125.
2. R. G. Lee, *Great Is the Lord* (Westwood, N.J.: Fleming H. Revell, 1955), 88.
3. Steve Brown in *Key Life Network* newsletter, Spring 1992, 8.

The Gospel Has No Boundaries

Background Passage: Acts 17:16–34
Focal Passage: Acts 17:22–34

A survey of the New Testament must include the expansion of the gospel recorded in the book of Acts. This book reflects the debate among Jewish Christians about whether the gospel should be offered to Gentiles without them first becoming Jews. Paul emerged as the strongest advocate for salvation by grace through faith, offered to all people. Acts 17:16–34 records his missionary work in Athens.

▶**Study Aim:** *To summarize Paul's sermon to the Athenians and their responses.*

STUDYING THE BIBLE

OUTLINE AND SUMMARY

    I. **Witnessing in Athens (Acts 17:16–21)**
        1. **In the synagogue and market (17:16–17)**
        2. **Confrontations with Greek philosophers (17:18–21)**
    II. **Preaching to the Athenians (Acts 17:22–34)**
        1. **Making known the unknown God (17:22–23)**
        2. **God as Creator and Lord (17:24–25)**
        3. **The Creator's purpose (17:26–29)**
        4. **Call to repent (17:30–31)**
        5. **Mixed responses (17:32–34)**

In Athens, Paul witnessed in the synagogue and in the marketplace (17:16–17). Greek philosophers were confused but curious about what Paul said (17:18–21). When Paul was invited to speak to the council, he began by referring to their altar to the unknown God (17:22–23). He made known this God as the Creator of all things (17:24–25). The Creator's purpose for humans was that people might seek Him (17:26–29). God raised Christ from the dead, and commands all to repent or face judgment (17:30–31). The Athenians responded with ridicule, procrastination, and faith (17:32–34).

I. Witnessing in Athens (Acts 17:16–21)

1. In the synagogue and market (17:16–17)

Paul was in Athens on his second missionary journey (Acts 15:36–18:22). Paul had left Timothy and Silas in Berea while he went on alone to Athens, the cultural center of the ancient world (17:10–15). Paul was angry when he found so many idols (17:16). He witnessed in the synagogue to the Jews and to the God-fearing Gentiles; he also went daily into the marketplace (17:17).

2. Confrontations with Greek philosophers (17:18–21)

In the marketplace, Paul encountered members of two prominent schools of Greek philosophy—Epicureans and Stoics. They misunderstood Paul's witness to "Jesus and the resurrection" to be the names of two gods (17:18). Therefore, they took Paul to a council called the Areopagus, where he could state his views to a larger group (17:19). The Athenians were curious about Paul's teaching, as they were about every new idea (17:20–21).

II. Preaching to the Athenians (Acts 17:22–34)
1. Making known the unknown God (17:22–23)

22 Then Paul stood in the midst of Mars' Hill, and said, Ye men of Athens, I perceive that in all things ye are too superstitious.

23 For as I passed by, and beheld your devotions, I found an altar with this inscription: TO THE UNKNOWN GOD. Whom therefore ye ignorantly worship, him declare I unto you.

The name *Areopagus* means "hill of Ares." The Greek god of war was Ares. His Roman name was Mars. Thus the name *Mars' Hill* comes from *Areopagus*. The Areopagus seems to have been both a council and the name of the place where it met. The invitation was an opportunity to preach to a crucial and hard-to-reach group.

The translation reads as if Paul began by calling his listeners ignorant and superstitious. The word translated "superstitious" can also mean "religious." The word translated "ignorantly" can mean "unknowingly." Paul said that he found them to be very religious—so religious in fact that they even had an altar to "THE UNKNOWN GOD." Apparently, the Greeks feared that they might have overlooked one of the gods, so they intended this altar to ensure that no god was ignored. Paul commended their desire to worship the unknown God. He told them that he intended to make known to them the God whom they sought to worship but did not yet know.

2. God as Creator and Lord (17:24–25)

24 God that made the world and all things therein, seeing that he is Lord of heaven and earth, dwelleth not in temples made with hands;

25 Neither is worshipped with men's hands, as though he needed any thing, seeing he giveth to all life, and breath, and all things.

Paul told them that the God who was unknown to them was the one and only God. He was Creator of all things and thus Lord of heaven and earth. This fact has two implications about worshiping God: (1) This one true God cannot be confined to earthly temples (see 1 Kings 8:22; Acts 7:48–50), and (2) God is not dependent on human gifts and sacrifices, but He Himself is the giver of every good and perfect gift (James 1:17). This included the gift of life itself. In popular Greek religion, people tried to get the favor of various gods by offerings and prayers.

3. The Creator's purpose (17:26–29)

> **26 And hath made of one blood all nations of men for to dwell on all the face of the earth, and hath determined the times before appointed, and the bounds of their habitation.**

God not only gave humans the gift of life, but He also created all people from one source. Apparently Paul had in mind Genesis 1–2, which sees all humanity descended from the first human pair. Differences in humans have happened since then, but all come from one source. This fact undercut the claim of the Greeks to be superior. They divided humanity into Greeks and barbarians. Even the Jews, who knew Genesis 1–2, divided humanity into Jews as God's chosen people and unclean Gentiles. Paul's point is that all humanity shares one Creator and sprang from one pair.

God not only created humanity, but He also continued to act within human history to accomplish His purpose. In the last part of verse 26, Paul talked about the epochs of history and the places of human settlement. These did not take place by mere chance but under God's oversight.

> **27 That they should seek the Lord, if haply they might feel after him, and find him, though he be not far from every one of us:**
>
> **28 For in him we live, and move, and have our being; as certain also of your own poets have said, For we are also his offspring.**
>
> **29 Forasmuch then as we are the offspring of God, we ought not to think that the Godhead is like unto gold, or silver, or stone, graven by art and man's device.**

God's purpose in creating humans was that people might come to know the Creator. Paul used the words "that they should seek the Lord" to say this. He did not mention by name God's creation of humans in His own image, but that was in His mind (Gen. 1:26–27).

Verse 27 hints that humanity failed to take advantage of this opportunity. The word *haply* means "perhaps." The word *feel* has the idea of "grope." In Romans 1:19–23, Paul said clearly that humanity had enough revelation of God in nature to see God's power; but they chose to reject that light and to turn from God to idolatry. Paul did not accuse the Athenians of this, but he implied that their gross idolatry showed that the closest they had come to finding God was their altar to the unknown God.

In spite of their failure to find God, Paul declared that the all powerful Creator is not far from any person. In fact, Paul quoted a Greek saying that we live and move and have our being in God. The Greeks, of course, did not mean by this the same thing that Paul meant. For example, the Stoics were pantheists. They believed that everything has a divine spark within it. Paul taught that God is separate from His creation, but that He seeks fellowship with those made in His own image.

Paul quoted a Greek poet as saying, "For we are also his offspring." These words were written by a Stoic poet named Aratus, who lived in the third century B.C. Aratus was thinking of Zeus, the chief god of the Greeks, and of humanity sharing in the divine nature of Zeus. Paul, of course, was thinking of the Lord God. We are His offspring in the sense of being created by Him in His image. Paul pointed out that this shows that God is not something that people make out of silver, gold, or wood. The true God created *us*—not the other way around. In idolatry, the people make their own gods and thus can control their gods. In the Bible, God creates people.

4. Call to repent (17:30–31)

30 And the times of this ignorance God winked at; but now commandeth all men every where to repent.

31 Because he hath appointed a day, in the which he will judge the world in righteousness by that man whom he hath ordained; whereof he hath given assurance unto all men in that he hath raised him from the dead.

The word translated "winked at" means "overlooked." God showed patient forbearance toward those who acted without clear knowledge. However, Paul declared that God has now so clearly revealed His purpose that He commands all people everywhere to repent. All must face judgment for their sins unless they heed God's call to turn from their sins. In that case, God will forgive their sins.

Verses 30–31 do not spell out all that Paul usually said on this subject. Verse 30, for example, does not make clear who the "man" is. Probably Paul was interrupted before he finished. On the other hand, remember that Paul had been witnessing to them in the marketplace about Jesus and the Resurrection (17:18). Therefore, they probably had already heard this part of Paul's sermon.

Paul based the assurance of all he said on the resurrection of Jesus Christ from the dead. Everything in verses 30–31 was foreign to the views of the Epicureans and Stoics, but especially the idea of bodily resurrection. Both groups were appalled at the idea that a body could be raised from the dead (see 1 Cor. 15:12). They were also offended at the call to repent and the threat of a day of judgment. The Epicureans believed that happiness is the main purpose of human life; therefore, they had little concern for morality. The Stoics believed in each person's ability to attain moral self-sufficiency.

5. Mixed Responses (17:32–34)

32 And when they heard of the resurrection of the dead, some mocked: and others said, We will hear thee again of this matter.

33 So Paul departed from among them.

34 Howbeit certain men clave unto him, and believed: among the which was Dionysius the Areopagite, and a woman named Damaris, and others with them.

Some of Paul's hearers sneered at his doctrine of resurrection (see Acts 26:23–26). Others asked to hear more. This may have been merely a way of rejecting (see Acts 24:24–27), or these may have been sincere seekers. Yet a third group believed. One of these, Dionysius, was a member of the council, thus an important convert. One woman convert is mentioned by name, and still others are referred to as a group.

Was Paul's work in Athens a failure? Many rejected his message, and only a few converts are named. We have no record in the Bible of a church at Athens. Some Bible students cite Paul's own words in 1 Corinthians 2:1–2 as evidence that Paul himself regretted the approach he had taken at Athens. According to this view, when Paul went from Athens to Corinth (Acts 18:1), he felt that he had failed in Athens because he had tried to use a philosophical approach rather than preaching Christ crucified.

However, in 1 Corinthians 2:1–2, Paul was not contrasting his preaching at Athens to his preaching at Corinth; he was contrasting his preaching to the worldly wisdom of Corinthian opponents. Paul often adapted his methods and approach to his audience (1 Cor. 9:19–22). Athens was not the only place where Paul preached God as Creator and Judge, repentance, and the resurrection of Christ (see Acts 14:15–17; 1 Thess. 1:9–10). And who can measure success in number of converts? Remember that Paul was preaching to the toughest kind of people to convince—dogmatic intellectuals. Remember that some believed, including a member of the council.

SUMMARY OF BIBLE TRUTHS

1. Although God is revealed in nature, many people turn from God to idolatry.
2. Missionaries try to make known the unknown God.
3. God is Creator and giver of all good things.
4. His purpose is that people come to know and serve Him.
5. God commands all to repent because judgment day is coming, a fact attested by Christ's resurrection.
6. Although some reject Christ and others put off a decision, some believe.

APPLYING THE BIBLE

1. "To the unknown god." The ancient city of Athens was full of altars to unknown gods. William Barclay tells how it all happened. It seems that about six hundred years before Paul's day, a pestilence hit the city. A poet from the island of Crete named Epimenides led the people to stay the plague by letting loose a flock of black and white sheep throughout the city. "Wherever each (sheep) lay down it was sacrificed to the nearest god; and if a sheep lay down near the shrine of no known god it was sacrificed to 'The Unknown God.' Paul took one of those altars as the starting place for his sermon.[1]

2. Ancient theories and their modern counterparts. What did the Epicureans and Stoics believe? The Epicureans, named for the philosopher Epicurus (341–270 B.C.), believed that all things happened by chance, that we are all subject to a blind determinism—that we have no true choices and that the good life is the pursuit of pleasure, of one sort or the other, after which we simply die and cease to be. The Stoics believed that a spark of the "divine" existed in every person but that humans could do nothing to change their lot; they must therefore accept whatever happened (whatever "the gods ordained") with a cool, calm and dispassionate equanimity, or as we say today, "stoically." The key idea was to face life's challenges with rationality, not the emotions. They sought the virtue expressed by William Ernest Henley's poem "Invictus": "I am the master of my fate; I am the captain of my soul." Discuss how these two ancient theories manifest themselves in the modern world.

3. Paul and the philosophers. In his sermon at Athens, Paul corrected errors about various philosophies and ideologies. He counteracted

- atheism, or the dogma that there is no God;
- pantheism, or the idea that everything is God and God is everything;
- materialism, or the notion that matter is eternal;
- fatalism, or the superstition that no intelligence presides over the universe;
- polytheism, or the notion that there are many gods;
- naturalism, or the ideology that man needs no further revelation than nature affords;
- henotheism, or the concept that "my god is good enough for me, but yours may be good enough for you";
- ritualism, or the belief that God is honored by purely external religious rites;
- evolutionism, or the hypothesis that man is a product of time and matter, apart from the act of a personal God;
- indifferentism, or the creed that God exists but does not care about man;
- optimism, or the belief that man has no sin, and that things are getting better and better in every way;
- unitarianism, or the teaching that Jesus was an ordinary man and not the Son of God;
- annihilationism, or the tenet that at death all people perish;
- universalism, or the teaching that all people will finally be saved, and
- determinism, or the theory that humans can do nothing whatever to change their lot, either in time or eternity.

4. The resurrection is our main argument. If you were a missionary like Paul, if you were to be able to preach only one sermon, what would the subject of that sermon be? Paul spoke of "Jesus and the resurrection" (Acts 17:18). And that was the final, clinching argument he made (at least as reported in our text, since we may not have the entire sermon) about the proof of God's supernatural activity in human history (Acts 17:31). What are the advantages of beginning and ending with that truth?

5. Was Paul successful at Athens? Some say that Paul was mistaken in his approach in this sermon because he quoted the pagan poets Aratus and Cleanthes in Acts 17:28. And that, when he wrote to Corinth, having "learned his lesson," he determined to know nothing but "Jesus Christ, and him crucified" (1 Cor. 2:2). Ask yourself these questions:

▶ Is it always a bad thing to quote a non-Christian when preaching God's truth?

▶ In view of the fact that some came to Christ, in your view, was Paul "unsuccessful"?

▶ How would you describe a "successful" witness for Christ.

▶ Would you characterize Noah as "unsuccessful"? (He won no converts.)

▶ Did Paul, in your view, give a faithful presentation of truth at Athens?

6. Calling others to repentance. Paul did not ask his hearers to think (as Stoics would have emphasized first) or to feel (as the Epicureans would have emphasized first), but to act. He said "but now (God) commandeth all men everywhere to repent" (Acts 17:30). Notice the words *all* and *everywhere*. Paul was an apologist for the gospel—he explained it rationally. But he was more than an apologist: He was an evangelist who called people to obey God and to obtain His salvation. As an apologist, a Christian explains, but as an evangelist, the Christian expects. The apologist uses the indicative; the evangelist uses the imperative. Discuss these questions: What right does a Christian have to call people, in the name of God, to repent and turn from their sins? Is repentance necessary today?

TEACHING THE BIBLE

▶ *Main Idea:* The gospel is for every person who has been born because God created all people.

▶ *Suggested Teaching Aim:* To lead adults not to place boundaries on the gospel.

A TEACHING OUTLINE

The Gospel Has No Boundaries

1. *Witnessing in Athens (Acts 17:16–21)*
2. *Preaching to the Athenians (Acts 17:22–34)*

Introduce the Bible Study

Tell this fable: One day two hand puppets—one named Stripes and one named Spots—got into an argument over which was better—stripes or spots. After arguing for some time, they discovered that the hands inside them were both linked to the same puppeteer and both were brought to life by him. Say: Our lesson today is a reminder that since God has made all of us, no one is excluded from the gospel. God loves all people and wants them to come to know Him; we should desire the same thing.

ch for Biblical Truth

lain that this lesson continues the survey of the New Testament. Witnessing in Athens" (Acts 17:16–21) on a chalkboard or a of paper. On a map of the New Testament world, locate Athens. Use the material on these verses in "Studying the Bible" to set the context. Use "Ancient theories and their modern counterparts" in "Applying the Bible" to explain who the Stoics and Epicureans were and what they believed.

Write "2. Preaching to the Athenians" on the chalkboard. Ask a member to read 17:22–23 aloud. Use the material in "Studying the Bible" to explain the reference to Mars' Hill/Areopagus and "THE UNKNOWN GOD."

Ask members to read 17:24–25 silently. Ask: What can we learn about God from these verses. (List members' suggestions on the chalkboard.) Ask, What implications about worshiping God do these facts suggest? (See "Studying the Bible.")

Ask members to read 17:26–29 silently. Ask: What implications does verse 26 have for race relations? (God created all races from one person.) For human history? (No one race is superior to another; God continues to act in human history.) Why did God create humans? (So they could know their Creator [v. 27].) Why have humans failed in knowing the Creator?

Ask members to read silently 17:30–31. Ask: Why has God chosen this time for all to repent? (In His wisdom He had sent Jesus.) Using the material in "Studying the Bible," explain why the concept of repentance and resurrection was so hard for the Epicureans and Stoics to accept.

Ask members to read silently 17:32–34 and to identify three groups who responded to Paul's preaching. (Scoffers, those who wanted more time, believers.)

Using the six statements in "Summary of Bible Truths," lecture briefly to sum up the basic teachings of today's lesson.

Give the Truth a Personal Focus

Before you read the following list, ask members to listen for those that would be welcomed in your church: college professor, Islamic immigrant, homeless person, Vietnamese refugee, factory worker, farmer, welfare recipient.

Ask: What boundaries has God placed on His gospel? (None.) What boundaries has our church—and we as individuals—placed on the gospel? Do we really believe the gospel is for everyone or those who are like us? List these on a chalkboard. Ask, What can we do to remove these boundaries? What will we do to remove them?

---

1. William Barclay, *The Acts of the Apostles* (Philadelphia: Westminster, 1976), 132.

Civic Responsibility

Background Passage: Romans 12:9–13:14
Focal Passage: Romans 13:1–14

The early Christians were under the dominion of two kingdoms. As believers, they were citizens of God's kingdom. They also were subjects of the Roman Empire. The situation was complicated by the mixed practice of protection and persecution of Christians by Rome. Christians were faced with the dilemma of being loyal to God's kingdom, while fulfilling their civic responsibility to Rome. Romans 13 contains the Bible's classic statement on this subject.

▶**Study Aim:** To identify their civic responsibilities in light of their ultimate loyalty to God's kingdom.

STUDYING THE BIBLE

OUTLINE AND SUMMARY
  I. **Christian Love in Action (Rom. 12:9–21)**
      1. **How love acts toward other Christians (12:9–13)**
      2. **How love acts toward all people (12:14–21)**
  II. **Citizens of Two Kingdoms (Rom. 13:1–14)**
      1. **Government divinely ordained (13:1–2)**
      2. **Purpose of civil government (13:3–4)**
      3. **Christian duties toward the state (13:5–7)**
      4. **Living by the law of love (13:8–10)**
      5. **Living by God's standards (13:11–14)**

Christians act in love toward one another in many ways (12:9–13). Believers also must act in love toward all people, even enemies (12:14–21). The idea of government is established by God (13:1–2). God's purpose for government is to maintain order and dispense justice (13:3–4). Christians owe the state to obey laws, pay taxes, and show proper respect (13:5–7). Christians live by love that requires more than law (13:8–10). As citizens of the coming kingdom, Christians refuse to participate in the evils of pagan society (13:11–14).

I. Christian Love in Action (Rom. 12:9–21)
1. How love acts toward other Christians (12:9–13)
Verses 9–13 contain twelve descriptions of how Christians are to practice love toward one another. Love has no pretense, and it stands for good and opposes evil (12:9). Within the family of faith, love displays brotherly affection; and it humbly honors other family members (12:10). It practices spiritual fervor in every aspect of life (12:11). Love is expressed in joyful hope, endurance of trials, and continual prayer (12:12). Love generously helps needy Christians and shows hospitality (12:13).

2. How love acts toward all people (12:14–21)

Romans 12:14, 19–21 focuses on love for enemies; 12:15–16 on fellow Christians; and 12:17–18 on all people. Christians bless rather than curse those who persecute them (12:14). They empathize with one another in joys and in sorrows (12:15). They practice harmony and humility toward one another (12:16). Christians live in such a way as to practice love and honesty toward unbelievers (12:17). They make every effort to live at peace with all kinds of people (12:18). Christians not only refuse to seek vengeance, but they also return good for evil (12:19–21).

II. Citizens of Two Kingdoms (Rom. 13:1–14)

1. Government divinely ordained (13:1–2)

1 Let every soul be subject unto the higher powers. For there is no power but of God: the powers that be are ordained of God.

2 Whosoever therefore resisteth the power, resisteth the ordinance of God: and they that resist shall receive to themselves damnation.

"Higher powers" and "powers that be" are words sometimes used for spiritual authorities and powers, but they are used here of earthly governments. "Ordained" means "established." That is, God Himself established the idea of earthly government. God did not ordain any particular form of government, but He is the author of communities organizing governments for maintaining order and security.

Verse 2 is stated strongly. Tyrants have often quoted verse 2 to justify their tyranny and to condemn any rebellion or revolution. Others have used it to condemn any form of dissent from the majority opinion, especially any form of civil disobedience. Paul did not discuss the matter of how to deal with governments that become tyrannical and demonic. (See comments on 13:5–7.)

2. Purpose of civil government (13:3–4)

3 For rulers are not a terror to good works, but to the evil. Wilt thou then not be afraid of the power? do that which is good, and thou shalt have praise of the same:

4 For he is the minister of God to thee for good. But if thou do that which is evil, be afraid; for he beareth not the sword in vain: for he is the minister of God, a revenger to execute wrath upon him that doeth evil.

These verses state the divinely appointed function of civil government. The state is to protect law-abiding citizens against criminals—thus maintaining order and stability. Paul even called a government official "a minister of God" when the official acts to fulfill God's purpose for government. Thus, those who make and enforce the law are acting as servants of God when they act for the good of the citizens and when they punish criminals. Individuals are not to take the law into their hands and seek revenge (12:19), but the state is to act for God in punishing criminals.

3. Christian duties toward the state (13:5–7)

5 Wherefore ye must needs be subject, not only for wrath, but also for conscience sake.

6 For for this cause pay ye tribute also: for they are God's ministers, attending continually upon this very thing.

7 Render therefore to all their dues: tribute to whom tribute is due; custom to whom custom; fear to whom fear; honour to whom honour.

Paul listed three duties of citizens:

1. to obey laws;
2. to pay taxes; and
3. to show proper respect.

Christians should obey the laws for the sake of conscience, not for fear of punishment. A society can remain stable only when most of the citizens obey the laws. There are not enough police to enforce laws in a society where most people break the laws.

Paul no doubt had in mind what Jesus said about paying taxes (Matt. 22:21). Followers of Christ owe ultimate obedience to God, but we also owe certain things to the civil government—one of which is paying taxes. Paul noted that taxes pay the expenses of the government in fulfilling its God-given functions.

Christians also owe proper respect to government officials, not because of who they are but because of the role they are ordained to play. Paul also prayed for the emperor that he might fulfill that role and maintain peace and order (1 Tim. 2:1–2).

Paul's summary of Christian duties leaves us with two unanswered questions:

1. How should Christians respond to a government that is tyrannical or that persecutes Christians?
2. What additional duties do Christians have in a free society?

The first-century Christians sought to obey and respect the government. However, the one exception was when some earthly authority called on them to disobey God. At such times, they followed the example of Peter and John, who put obedience to God first (Acts 5:29). However, they were careful to show that they were law-abiding citizens. They did this to counteract the pagans' slanders against them (see also 1 Pet. 2:13–17; 3:14–17). After all, Jesus was crucified on the false charge of sedition (Luke 23:2, 38), and the early Christians were often subjected to the same kind of false accusations (Acts 16:21).

During Paul's lifetime, the Roman government had a mixed response to Christians. The state often protected Paul against false charges (Acts 18:14–17; 19:35–41; 21:27–40; 23:12–35). However, ironically under Nero, Christians were persecuted in Rome; and strong tradition says that Paul and Peter were put to death by Nero, for whom Paul had prayed in 1 Timothy 2:2.

As for the other question, American Christians have opportunities to influence government that Paul never had. His influence had to be restricted to obeying the law, paying taxes, respecting officials, praying for them, preaching the gospel, nonparticipation in evils, and exemplifying a different way of living. However, we can do much more in a free society. We can exercise our rights to express our views, to vote, to run for office, to choose civil service as a vocation, and to fulfill many other civil roles.

4. Living by the law of love (13:8–10)

8 Owe no man any thing, but to love one another: for he that loveth another hath fulfilled the law.

9 For this, Thou shalt not commit adultery, Thou shalt not kill, Thou shalt not steal, Thou shalt not bear false witness, Thou shalt not covet; and if there be any other commandment, it is briefly comprehended in this saying, namely, Thou shalt love thy neighbour as thyself.

10 Love worketh no ill to his neighbour: therefore love is the fulfilling of the law.

Verse 8 returns to the theme of love in Romans 12:9–21, but it also relates to civic responsibility. The mention of owing taxes in verse 7 suggested another more important debt. Christians are obligated to love others. Some see verse 8 as denying ever going in debt, but Paul's point was to pay your debts. He then moved from that to a debt that we can never fully pay—loving others.

Verses 9–10 reflect the Ten Commandments and Jesus' use of Leviticus 19:18 (Mark 12:31). Love for our neighbors fulfills the law. Paul quoted from the commandments having to do with human relations. If we love our neighbors, we will not commit these sins against them. In fact, love demands far more than not stealing from our neighbors; it demands that we do good toward them.

Applied to civic responsibility, verses 8–10 reinforce earlier words about obeying the laws. However, the love commandment calls on Christians not only to live by the highest moral standards but also to treat others in ways that reflect the Golden Rule.

5. Living by God's standards (13:11–14)

11 And that, knowing the time, that now it is high time to awake out of sleep: for now is our salvation nearer than when we believed.

12 The night is far spent, the day is at hand: let us therefore cast off the works of darkness, and let us put on the armour of light.

13 Let us walk honestly, as in the day; not in rioting and drunkenness, not in chambering and wantonness, not in strife and envying.

14 But put ye on the Lord Jesus Christ, and make not provision for the flesh, to fulfill the lusts thereof.

The New Testament describes salvation as past, present, and future. We have been saved from sin's penalty; we are being saved from sin's power; we shall be saved from sin's presence. Romans 13:11–14 looks toward the future day of salvation. For Paul, this was not just a doctrine to believe but a call to present action. Those who are in the process of being saved do not just wait with folded hands for the future salvation. Relying on the Spirit's power, they seek to narrow the gap between what they are and what God has called them to be (Phil. 3:12–14).

The day of salvation is drawing nearer; therefore, Christians need to wake up and put on the armor of light. This means that they will live decently and reject the sins of the flesh. Paul listed three pairs of these: carousing ("rioting") and drunkenness, sexual immorality ("chambering") and shameless behavior ("wantonness"), strife and envy. All of these were typical of the sins of a lost world (Rom. 1:18–32) and had no place in the lives of Christians. Because many Christians had once lived this way and still lived where these sins flourished, they needed to resist these temptations.

Although Paul did not apply verses 11–14 directly to civic responsibility, they illustrate how Christians can contribute to earthly society by being loyal to heaven's standards. First-century Christians had no political clout, but they had the influence of their actions and words. By refusing to participate in these sins, they delivered a strong message to pagan society.

SUMMARY OF BIBLE TRUTHS

1. *Civil government is ordained by God to maintain order and dispense justice.*
2. *Christians have duties to their earthly nation, but their ultimate loyalty is to God and His kingdom.*
3. *Christians should obey the laws, pay taxes, and show proper respect.*
4. *Christians influence government by nonparticipation in evils and by living by the law of love.*

APPLYING THE BIBLE

1. Kingdoms in conflict. Chuck Colson was once asked, after becoming a Christian: "Mr. Colson, how can you try to live by the Sermon on the Mount and at the same time support the use of military might?" That question puts the issue in focus: What do we do when the virtues and values of the two kingdoms of our lives come into conflict, or at least apparent conflict? In 1987 Colson wrote a book entitled *Kingdoms in Conflict* with the subtitle "An insider's challenging view of politics, power, and the pulpit." That could serve as the title and subtitle of this lesson.[1]

2. How involved should I be in politics? Christians can live at two extremes: copping out of the political processes on the one hand, or becoming so immersed in them that they become an end-all solution to all problems. The pursuit of balance is the key, always maintaining the supremacy of the kingdom of God. James Dunn said: "When you decide not to be involved in politics, you have voted wrong. You will pay in the form of bad government and bad laws. We must get into politics. Common sense demands it. We must mix politics and religion." He added, "Since it is inevitable that we will mix religion, we ought to do it by the Christian rule of thumb and apply Christian principles to our roles as citizens."[2]

3. Romans 13:11–14 changed Augustine's life forever. Augustine was in deep distress because of his sin. Although on the brink of turning his life over to God, he couldn't bring himself to do so. He was walking about in a garden, weeping over his sins and talking to himself when he heard a voice saying, "Pick up (the book) and read it; pick it up and read it." He thought it was the voice of a child, perhaps in a game of some sort. He hurried back to a seat where his friend Alypius was sitting, and where Augustine had been reading some passages from Paul. "I seized it, opened it and immediately read in silence the paragraph on which my eyes first fell: '. . . not in the ways of banqueting and drunkenness, in immoral living and sensualities, passion and revelry, but clothe yourself in the Lord Jesus Christ, and make no plans to glut the body's lusts . . .' I did not want to read on. There was no need. Instantly at the end of this sentence, as if a light of confidence had been poured into my heart, all the darkness of my doubt fled away." It was for Augustine, a deliverance from one kingdom into another. Later, he was to write his famous *City of God,* in which he contrasted the glorious city of Rome, which had fallen, with the City of God, which was never to fall. His challenge was the same as ours: to live in both cities in a responsible way.[3]

4. Apathy is dangerous. Thomas Carlyle, "asking who was responsible for the horrors of the French Revolution, said every man in France—every man was to be blamed who in one way or another had come short of his public duty."[4]

5. Don't get involved in politics? I heard about some youngsters, somewhere in Maryland, circulating copies of the Bill of Rights as a petition. They asked over one hundred of their neighbors to sign it. More than half refused, and some said it was unpatriotic!

6. Discussion starters. Comment on the following sentiments:
- "Nothing is politically right which is morally wrong."[5]
- "Our country right or wrong. When right, to be kept right; when wrong, to be put right" (Carl Schurz).[6] What standard of judgment should Christians use to judge as to whether a nation is right or wrong?
- "Neutrality in politics is rebellion against the Lord Christ."[7] Can Christians take neutral positions on current moral issues?
- "The political involvement of evangelicals (is) 'history;' they're finished."[8] If evangelicals are "finished," it might be because they do not vote! It has been reported in various places that approximately 20 percent of evangelical voters actually vote; is that acceptable? Why?
- Stephen Douglas was very upset when he heard ministers arguing against the institution of slavery; in fact, he said that they were trying to coerce Congress in the name of Almighty God! Should ministers of Douglas's day have spoken out against slavery? Why?[9]

TEACHING THE BIBLE

- *Main Idea:* Christians' citizenship in heaven should make us the best citizens on earth.

▶ *Suggested Teaching Aim:* To lead adults to identify their civic responsibilities in light of their ultimate loyalty to God's kingdom.

A TEACHING OUTLINE

Civic Responsibility

1. *Government Divinely Ordained (Rom. 13:1–2)*
2. *Purpose of Civil Government (Rom. 13:13:3–4)*
3. *Christian Duties Toward the State (Rom. 13:5–7)*
4. *Living by the Law of Love (Rom. 13:8–10)*
5. *Living by God's Standards (13:11–14)*

Introduce the Bible Study

IN ADVANCE, secure a container of oil and water. Mark each clearly. Introduce the lesson by pouring the two into a small jar. Ask, What happens when I pour oil and water together? Then shake the jar and wait until the oil and water separate. Say: Some would say that government and religion are like oil and water—they do not mix. But that is not a biblical understanding of government and religion.

Search for Biblical Truth

IN ADVANCE, write the five points of "A Teaching Outline" on large strips of paper and tape to the backs of five chairs. Ask the person with point 1 to tape the strip to the focal wall. Ask members to open their Bibles to Romans 13 and read verses 1 and 2. Ask: What particular form of government did God establish? (None.) Is verse 2 always to be obeyed? Did Peter and the other apostles obey verse 2 (Acts 5:17–29)?

Ask the person with the second outline point to place it on the wall. Ask, According to verses 3–4, what is the purpose of the state? (Protect law-abiding citizens and punish evildoers.) Are individuals ever to take the law into their own hands? Why?

Ask the person with the third outline point to place it on the wall. Ask: Based upon verses 5–7, how are Christians to relate to the state? (Obey laws, pay taxes, show proper respect.) Ask: How should Christians respond to a government that is tyrannical or that persecutes Christians? What additional duties do Christians have in a free society? Write the following chart on a chalkboard (You may think of additional items to list):

Participation in Government		
Paul	Opportunity	Today
Express views		
Vote		
Run for office		
Choose civil service as vocation		

Ask members to answer *yes* or *no* for each of these. (Paul could participate only to a limited degree in the last one.) Ask: If Paul had no participation in the government, why did he urge support of it?

Ask the person with the fourth outline point to place it on the wall. Ask: How do Paul's words in verses 8–10 fit in with his discussion of government?

Ask the person with the fifth outline point to place it on the wall. Ask: What should prompt Christians to live exemplary lives? What does it mean to "put on the Lord Jesus Christ"? Read this statement: "First-century Christians had no political clout, but they had the influence of their actions and words. By refusing to participate in these sins, they delivered a strong message to pagan society."

Give the Truth a Personal Focus

Read James Dunn's statement in "How involved should I be in politics?" in "Applying the Bible." Hold up the jar of oil and water. Say: Religion and government are not oil and water. We must be involved as Christians. This may mean that Christians will be on different sides of the issues, but we must respect each other's views. The important thing is that we identify our civic responsibilities in light of our ultimate loyalty to God's kingdom.

---

1. Charles Colson, *Kingdoms in Conflict* (Grand Rapids: Zondervan, 1989).

2. Quoted in *Alabama Baptist,* 4/20/89, p. 6.

3. *The Confessions of St. Augustine,* tr. E. M. Blaiklock (Nashville: Thomas Nelson, 1983), 204.

4. Herbert Butterfield, *Christianity and History* (London: Collins, 1949), 53.

5. C. Henry Lewis, *Best Quotations for All Occasions* (Greenwich, Conn.: Fawcett Publications, 1961), 179.

6. *Bartlett's Familiar Quotations,* eleventh edition (Boston: Little, Brown, 1938), 580.

7. From *Biblical Principles* (Plymouth, Mass.: Plymouth Rock Foundation, 1984), 228.

8. Os Guiness and John Seel, *No God But God* (Chicago: Moody Press, 1992), 49.

9. Archbishop Desmund Tuto quoted by Charles Colson in *Kingdoms in Conflict* (Grand Rapids: Zondervan, 1987), 277.

Caring Community

Background Passage: 1 Corinthians 11:17–34
Focal Passage: 1 Corinthians 11:20–34

God intends for the church to be a caring community. Selfishness and pride thwart this purpose, but self-giving love fulfills it. This is the basic message of 1 Corinthians, written by Paul to a church riddled with problems. This lesson focuses on the problem of abuses of the fellowship meal and the Lord's Supper.

▶**Study Aim:** *To describe the abuses of the Lord's Supper in Corinth and how Paul responded.*

STUDYING THE BIBLE

OUTLINE AND SUMMARY

    I. **Abuses of the Lord's Supper (1 Cor. 11:17–22)**

   II. **Purposes of the Lord's Supper (1 Cor. 11:23–26)**

        1. "In remembrance of me" (11:23–25)

        2. Until He comes (11:26)

  III. **Participating in the Lord's Supper (1 Cor. 11:27–34)**

        1. Examine yourself (11:27–29)

        2. Chastised for sins (11:30–32)

        3. Participate together (11:33–34)

Shaming the poor at the Lord's Supper is a sin of despising the church of God (11:17–22). Jesus instituted the Lord's Supper to be taken in remembrance of Him (11:23–25). It also proclaims the Lord's death until He comes (11:26). In order not to take the Lord's Supper unworthily, Christians should engage in self-examination (11:27–29). Abuses of the Lord's Supper result in chastisements for Christians (11:30–32). Therefore, the richer members should wait for the poorer members (11:33–34).

I. Abuses of the Lord's Supper (1 Cor. 11:17–22)

20 When ye come together therefore into one place, this is not to eat the Lord's supper.

21 For in eating every one taketh before other his own supper: and one is hungry, and another is drunken.

22 What? have ye not houses to eat and to drink in? or despise ye the church of God, and shame them that have not? What shall I say to you? shall I praise you in this? I praise you not.

After Paul left Corinth (Acts 18:1–18), he received reports from several sources (1 Cor. 1:11; 16:17–18). The church also wrote Paul and asked several specific questions (7:1). Paul wrote 1 Corinthians to answer the questions and to deal with the problems that had been reported to him. Whenever possible, Paul affirmed the Corinthian church (11:2); but he also rebuked them when they needed it (11:17). Divisions in the church was a problem that drew Paul's fire—whether arguments over leaders (1:10–13) or abuses of the Lord's Supper (11:18). If dissension has any good result at all, it is to reveal those who are genuine (11:19).

Some sincere readers of the Bible think that 1 Corinthians 11:20–22 teaches that Christians should not eat in the church building. However, the New Testament clearly shows that eating together was a good way of expressing Christian fellowship and caring for the needs of the poor (Acts 2:46; Gal. 2:12). These meals were sometimes called love (*agape*) feasts (2 Pet. 2:13; Jude 12). First Corinthians 11:17–34 shows that they often took the Lord's Supper as part of a fellowship meal. This seemed normal to them since the Lord instituted the supper at an actual meal with His disciples.

What Paul rebuked was not the fellowship meal or combining it with the Lord's Supper. He condemned the selfish and insensitive way in which some of the richer members of the church acted. Judging from verses 20–22, one of two things or a combination of these was happening. They may have eaten their own ample food without sharing it with the poorer members. More likely, in light of the word *tarry* in verse 33, the wealthier members arrived early and ate before the poorer members could arrive.

Taking the Lord's Supper was a farce under such conditions. The poorer members were left hungry, and some of the richer members were not only stuffed but drunk (11:21). Paul charged them with the twofold sin of despising the church of God and shaming the poor.

We call "them that have not" the "have-nots" or the poor. The Bible shows that God has a special concern for this group. The church was supposed to be a family of the loving heavenly Father, in which all the brothers and sisters stood on equal footing. The usual distinctions by which the world ranks and divides people should not be in God's family. Yet wealthier family members were totally ignoring and thus shaming their poorer brothers and sisters. Paul said that such a sin despises the church of God. This is inconsistent with faith in the Lord of glory (James 2:1–8).

II. Purposes of the Lord's Supper (1 Cor. 11:23–26)

1. "In remembrance of me" (11:23–25)

23 For I have received of the Lord that which also I delivered unto you, That the Lord Jesus the same night in which he was betrayed took bread:

24 And when he had given thanks, he brake it, and said, Take, eat: this is my body, which is broken for you: this do in remembrance of me.

25 After the same manner also he took the cup, when he had supped, saying, This cup is the new testament in my blood: this do ye, as oft as ye drink it, in remembrance of me.

Since Paul wrote this letter before the Gospels were put into written form, this is the earliest New Testament record of the institution of the Lord's Supper. Paul had not made this up. He was delivering to the

Corinthians what he had received from the Lord and others about what happened on the night of His betrayal. These words are the keys to God's purposes for the Lord's Supper.

Since Jesus repeated the words "in remembrance of me," this is a primary clue to God's purpose. The Jewish Christians were familiar with the Passover meal, which commemorated the deliverance from Egypt. Since they saw Christ as their Passover Lamb (1 Cor. 5:7), they saw the Lord's Supper as a memorial of a past deliverance. The blood of Jesus was shed at the cross for salvation from sin. "In remembrance of me" means more than a memorial of deliverance. Jesus the Lord conquered death. They were to remember not only what He did for them; they were to remember Him. The Lord's Supper is a communion with the living Lord (1 Cor. 10:16–17).

The words "this is my body" have been understood in a variety of ways. Some of us have strongly resisted the doctrine that Christ is physically present in the elements of the supper. However, we need to affirm where He is present. He is present in and among us.

2. Until He comes (11:26)

26 For as often as ye eat this bread, and drink this cup, ye do shew the Lord's death till he come.

"Shew" means "proclaim." The Lord's Supper has a past, a present, and a future dimension. We proclaim His future coming. Jesus spoke about not eating again with the disciples until the future heavenly feast (Matt. 26:29; Mark 14:25; Luke 22:16, 18). Thus the supper inspires confident hope of participating in the joys of the wonderful future that God is preparing for His people.

III. Participating in the Lord's Supper (1 Cor. 11:27–34)

1. Examine yourself (11:27–29)

27 Wherefore whosoever shall eat this bread, and drink this cup of the Lord, unworthily, shall be guilty of the body and blood of the Lord.

28 But let a man examine himself, and so let him eat of that bread, and drink of that cup.

29 For he that eateth and drinketh unworthily, eateth and drinketh damnation to himself, not discerning the Lord's body.

A common misunderstanding of these verses is to assume that Paul is denying the Lord's Supper to anyone who feels unworthy. If that were true, none of us could partake, for we are all unworthy sinners. Paul was not speaking of unworthy people, but of taking the Lord's Supper in an unworthy manner.

How might someone take it "unworthily"? Paul had already identified one way to commit this sin. The actions of the rich Corinthians who ate before the poorer members were condemned by Paul because they despised the church of God by shaming the poor (11:20–22). Thus, when anyone takes the Lord's Supper while acting selfishly and indifferently to fellow church members, he takes the supper unworthily.

Verse 29 warns against failing to "discern the Lord's body." This can mean at least two things: (1) One possibility is to take the Lord's Supper carelessly or irreverently. This ignores and profanes the sacred meaning of the Lord's death for us. (2) Another possible meaning is to assume that "body" refers to the church as Christ's body (1 Cor. 12:12). Paul may have been thinking of those who take the Lord's Supper while ignoring, hurting, or holding grudges against fellow church members.

The Corinthian offenders were guilty of both. They ignored and hurt their poorer brothers, with whom the Lord identifies (Matt. 25:34–40). And they apparently turned the fellowship meal and thus the Lord's Supper into a party, perhaps even a drunken orgy. Paul used strong language to describe the seriousness of this sin: "guilty of the body and blood of Christ." In verse 29, he spoke of "damnation," although the word he used is the general word for "judgment."

In verses 30–32, Paul tried to assume the best—that these were genuine Christians whom the Lord was chastening, not that they were lost sinners. On the other hand, he used language that did not rule out that some of them might not be true followers of the Lord.

In order to avoid taking the Lord's Supper unworthily, Paul said that each participant needs to prepare by a self-examination. This examination is designed to uncover any unconfessed sins, any hostile feelings toward fellow church members, and any irreverence toward the Lord. The word translated "examine" means to put to the test in order to prove the genuineness of something. Thus, it implies that if self-examination reveals something wrong, the genuine Christian will set it right before partaking.

2. Chastised for sins (11:30–32)

30 For this cause many are weak and sickly among you, and many sleep.

31 For if we would judge ourselves, we should not be judged.

32 But when we are judged, we are chastened of the Lord, that we should not be condemned with the world.

Some people believe that any trouble someone experiences is punishment for some sin. The book of Job and Jesus' words in John 9:1–3 show that not all suffering is the direct result of our sins; however, 1 Corinthians 11:30–32 shows that sometimes suffering is punishment for sin (see also John 5:14). Paul wrote that some of the Corinthian offenders were sick, some were weak, and some had died as punishment for such sins. Paul, however, made it clear that when this happens to a genuine Christian, the punishment is the chastening hand of a loving Father (Heb. 12:5–9), not condemnation to hell.

Verse 31 is a plea that we judge ourselves, lest God do it for us. This is the same idea in the call to examine yourself. Examine yourself and make changes, lest you be chastened by the Lord, or—what is worse—lest you show yourself not a true believer and thus face condemnation along with the world.

3. Participate together (11:33–34)

33 Wherefore, my brethren, when ye come together to eat, tarry one for another.

34 And if any man hunger, let him eat at home; that ye come not together unto condemnation. And the rest will I set in order when I come.

Notice that Paul called them "my brethren." In spite of their sins, he was assuming the best of them. This is why he interpreted their punishments as chastisements of a loving Father rather than condemnation of lost sinners.

Paul addressed himself again to the problem mentioned in 11:20–22. He told the rich to wait patiently for their poorer brothers before eating. Those who were too hungry to wait ought to eat something at home rather than shaming the poor. The reason for waiting was that the poorer members worked longer hours and could not assemble together as early as the more affluent. Many of them were slaves who were forced to work seven long days each week. The first day of the week was just another day so far as their pagan masters were concerned.

Paul planned to visit Corinth in the near future. He promised to deal with anyone who ignored his clear words in this letter.

SUMMARY OF BIBLE TRUTHS

1. Each church should be a family of faith and love.
2. Selfishness and pride thwart this divine purpose, but self-giving love fulfills it.
3. The Lord's Supper means gratitude for past deliverance, communion with the living Lord, and proclamation of future hope.
4. Christian's should engage in self-examination to avoid taking the Lord's Supper in an unworthy way.
5. Shaming poorer church members is a way of despising the church of God.
6. God chastises His children who commit such sins.

APPLYING THE BIBLE

1. Honoring the Lord's Supper. I once was asked by a member of a pulpit committee if I "tacked the Lord's Supper on" to the end of the service. I assured him that I always tried to make the experience the focus of the entire service, planning the event with some care, and giving it the emphasis that our Lord and the early disciples did. One well-known theologian says that the Lord's Supper is "the summit of Christian experience." Ask these questions:

▶ Which took precedence for the disciples on the night before the Crucifixion: the Passover meal or the Lord's Supper?

▶ What are some ways we trivialize the Lord's Supper?

2. How do we sin against the Lord's Supper? The Corinthians were insensitive in observing the Lord's Supper and abused it in various ways, some of which are difficult to identify precisely:

(1) Divisions. Our English word *schism* comes from the Greek word *schismata*, which is used in 1 Corinthians 11:18 to refer to divisions that were allowed to continue in the church.

(2) Factions. The Greek word *haireseis* is translated "heresies" in 1 Corinthians 11:19. It refers to various factions that dominated the assembly.

(3) Selfishness. Some ate to the full while others went hungry (1 Cor. 11:21).

(4) Drunkenness. Some were actually drunk (1 Cor. 11:21).

(5) Insensitivity. The poor were shamed (1 Cor. 11:22).

(6) Unworthy participation. Some ate in an "unworthy" manner (1 Cor. 11:27).

(7) Carelessness. Some ate without self-examination, perhaps the most flagrant sin (1 Cor. 11:27).

(8) Impatience with others. Apparently, some were noticeably impatient with others (1 Cor. 11:33).

It is not clear what "and if any man hunger, let him eat at home" means, but it probably had to do with the rich flaunting their wealth (1 Cor. 11:34). Does all this apply in any way to modern churches when we partake of the supper? How do we sin against the supper?

3. Names for the Lord's Supper. The Lord's Supper has gone by various names:

▶ *The Lord's Supper.* That exact phrase is used in 1 Corinthians 11:20. The fact that the meal was at supper time is also mentioned in Mark 14:17.

▶ *Communion.* Our Lord chose to commune with His followers in the experience, and to encourage their communion with each other. "The cup of blessing which we bless, is it not a participation (Greek koinonia=communion, fellowship) in the body of Christ?" (1 Cor. 10:16).

▶ *Eucharist.* The Greek word *eucharistein* means "to give thanks," as Jesus did (Matt. 26:26–27, etc.). This word is used in 1 Corinthians 14:16, and some use it as a title for the Lord's Supper.

▶ *Mass.* Catholics use this word in reference to what we call the Lord's Supper, but we see the supper in an altogether different light than they do. The Catholic doctrine of *transubstantiation* teaches that the wine and wafer are literally transformed into the blood and body of the Lord. (The word *mass* is from a Latin phrase with which the priest ends the ceremony, "Ite, missa est," which simply means, "Go, you are dismissed." The phrase and the word *mass,* from which it derives, has nothing to do with the biblical account of the supper.)

4. Discussion questions:

▶ Should persons abstain from participating in the supper because they are imperfect, to avoid eating and drinking "unworthily"?

▶ How often should churches observe the Lord's Supper? The New Testament makes no reference to the matter; Paul does say "as oft as you eat this bread and drink this cup" (1 Cor. 11:26).

> All meals, to the ancients, were seen as communion with the gods (or with God) who gave the food (thus prayers) and as an act of communion with those who were eating (and as an exclusion of others). How does all that apply to the body of Christ in this meal setting?

> If a church member were at odds with another church member and asked your counsel about eating the supper, what would your counsel be?

> I once had a pastor friend who argued vehemently for observing the supper only in evening services. Do you agree? Why?

TEACHING THE BIBLE

> *Main Idea:* A caring community will observe the Lord's Supper properly.

> *Suggested Teaching Aim:* To lead adults to observe the Lord's Supper in a proper manner.

A TEACHING OUTLINE

Caring Community

1. *Abuses of the Lord's Supper (1 Cor. 11:17–22)*
2. *Purposes of the Lord's Super (1 Cor. 11:23–26)*
3. *Participating in the Lord's Supper (1 Cor. 11:27–34)*

Introduce the Bible Study

Get a Lord's Supper juice cup and bread plate or use a goblet and a loaf of bread to create interest. Sing or read the words to the hymn, "In Remembrance" (No. 365, *The Baptist Hymnal,* 1991). Ask, What other ministries does this hymn link with the Lord's Supper? (Feed the poor, heal the sick, let brother in.) Are these ministries legitimate to link with the Lord's Supper? Say, Today's lesson will help us learn how to observe the Lord's Supper properly.

Search for Biblical Truth

On a chalkboard or large sheet of paper, write: "1. Abuses of the Lord's Supper (1 Cor. 11:17–22)." Use a map of the New Testament to locate Corinth. Ask members to read verses 17–22 silently. Lecture briefly, covering these points: (1) The New Testament churches often ate meals together (sometimes called "love feasts") and then observed the Lord's Supper after the meal—much the way Jesus did with His disciples the night before His death; (2) wealthy members arrived before the poorer members and started eating and even getting drunk; (3) the poor were shamed and embarrassed because they had nothing to eat; (4) this was not the proper atmosphere for observing the Lord's Supper.

On the chalkboard, write: "2. Purposes of the Lord's Supper (1 Cor. 11:23–26)." Ask members to read these verses silently. On a chalkboard, write: *Past, Present,* and *Future* at the top of three columns. Suggest that the supper has these three dimensions. Ask: What do we do that emphasizes the past when we observe the Lord's Supper? (Remember Jesus, the Passover Lamb.) What do we do that emphasizes the future? (Proclaim His future return.)

On the chalkboard, write: "3. Participating in the Lord's Supper (1 Cor. 11:27–34)." Ask: What do we do that emphasizes the present when we observe the supper? (Examine ourselves so we do not eat unworthily.) How can we observe the supper in an unworthy manner? (See "How do we sin against the Lord's Supper?" in "Applying the Bible" for a discussion of eight ways.) Why should we judge ourselves and change our behavior? (If we don't, God will judge and punish us.) Read this translation of verse 33: "You should wait until everyone gets there before you start eating" (CEV). Point out that Paul comes back to his original complaint against them that he had made in verse 21.

IN ADVANCE, copy the six statements in "Summary of Bible Truths" on six small strips of paper. Give these to six members to read in order at this time.

Give the Truth a Personal Focus

Distribute paper and pencils to all members. Read the list of "How do we sin against the Lord's Supper" slowly. Ask members to consider if they have sinned against the Lord's Supper by any of these methods.

Read this case study: "Virginia and Caroline (or George and Fred if you teach men) had been friends for years. However, Caroline had unknowingly hurt Virginia's feelings. Since she had not done it intentionally, she did not feel she owed Virginia an apology. Virginia had vowed not to speak to Caroline until she apologized. They both showed up in church the morning the Lord's Supper was being observed. When they saw that the supper was to be served, they . . ." Ask several members to suggest what the women should do. Read the Main Idea and close in prayer.

Reconciling the World to Christ

Background Passage: 2 Corinthians 5:11–21
Focal Passage: 2 Corinthians 5:11–21

Reconciliation is a familiar word in human relations. The Bible uses the same word to describe what happens when God reconciles sinners to Himself. After believers have been reconciled, God entrusts us with the ministry of calling others to be reconciled.

▶**Study Aim:** *To evaluate personal motives and practices in being ambassadors for Christ.*

STUDYING THE BIBLE

OUTLINE AND SUMMARY
- I. **Motives for Ministry (2 Cor. 5:11–15)**
  - 1. **Personal accountability to God (5:11)**
  - 2. **Concern for others (5:12–13)**
  - 3. **Love of Christ (5:14–15)**
- II. **Ministry of Reconciliation (2 Cor. 5:16–21)**
  - 1. **A new creation (5:16–17)**
  - 2. **Reconciled and reconciling (5:18–20)**
  - 3. **Good news for sinners (5:21)**

Christians are motivated by personal accountability to God (5:11), concern for others (5:12–13), and the love of Christ (5:14–15). Christians are new creations who see everything differently than they once did (5:16–17). God in Christ reconciles sinners to Himself and entrusts to them the ministry of reconciliation (5:18–20). Christ, who had no sin of His own, bore our sins so we can be declared righteous by God (5:21).

I. Motives for Ministry (2 Cor. 5:11–15)
1. Personal accountability to God (5:11)

11 Knowing therefore the terror of the Lord, we persuade men; but we are made manifest unto God; and I trust also are made manifest in your consciences.

On the surface, we might think the first part of this verse described Paul's zeal in trying to persuade sinners to repent before they face divine wrath (see 2 Cor. 5:20). However, 2 Corinthians 5:11b–13 and the book as a whole show that Paul meant something else in 5:11a. The fear of the Lord describes his accountability to God. He had just described how each of us must appear before the judgment seat of Christ (5:10). Paul did not mean that his salvation was in doubt; he did mean that he wanted to please the Lord in all things (5:9).

Paul wrote 2 Corinthians because he had been under attack by opponents in the Corinthian church. Much of the letter, therefore, is a defense of his ministry. He wanted to persuade the Corinthians that he was sincere in his determination to please the Lord. Paul told them that this fact was already known by God. His hope was that the Corinthians would also recognize this to be true.

2. Concern for others (5:12–13)

12 For we commend not ourselves again unto you, but give you occasion to glory on our behalf, that ye may have somewhat to answer them which glory in appearance, and not in heart.

13 For whether we be beside ourselves, it is to God: or whether we be sober, it is for your cause.

Paul wanted to give his friends in Corinth help in defending him against his critics. These critics looked on the outward appearance and not on the heart. The words "beside ourselves" and "sober" probably reflect two contrasting criticisms of Paul. Some of his critics accused him of being crazy. Others accused him of being too restrained—not spiritual enough to show his emotions.

The keys to Paul's reply to these critics are the words "to God" and "for your cause." Paul's actions were motivated by his commitment to serve God and by his concern for the Corinthians.

3. Love of Christ (5:14–15)

14 For the love of Christ constraineth us; because we thus judge, that if one died for all, then were all dead:

15 And that he died for all, that they which live should not henceforth live unto themselves, but unto him which died for them, and rose again.

Paul was motivated not only by personal accountability to God and by concern for others but also by the amazing love of Christ for himself and other sinners. "Constraineth" translates a word that means being hemmed in on both sides, thus being forced to move forward. Paul was restricted from the kind of self-seeking that put himself first. Instead he was led forward to living for Christ. The last part of verse 15 thus clarifies what he was constrained toward.

In between is Paul's description of the results of the love of Christ in dying for sinners. Christ died for all. In dying for sinners, he did two things:

1. He died the death sinners deserve in order that sinners might not have to die (see 5:21).
2. He died so that His abiding presence might enable saved sinners to die to self and sin.

Both are either stated or implied in verse 14. The words translated "therefore all were dead" are true, but most translations read "therefore all died." This death to sin is what Paul described in passages like Romans 6:2 and Galatians 2:20.

The cross thus not only saved Paul from the penalty of sin, but it also provided motivation and power to live a new kind of life. People who have experienced the presence and power of the crucified and risen Lord can no longer live for themselves. Now we are constrained to live for the One who died and was raised from the dead on our behalf.

II. Ministry of Reconciliation (2 Cor. 5:16–21)

1. A new creation (5:16–17)

16 Wherefore henceforth know we no man after the flesh: yea, though we have known Christ after the flesh, yet now henceforth know we him no more.

17 Therefore if any man be in Christ, he is a new creature: old things are passed away; behold, all things are become new.

Verse 16 is an example of the new outlook Paul had as a Christian. Prior to becoming a follower of Christ, Paul lived according to the standards of a world without Christ. Paul often described such living as life according to the flesh. Like most non-Christians, Paul judged things by outward appearances and by worldly standards of success. He even looked at Jesus Christ through eyes of flesh. That explains why he would lead a vicious persecution against the Son of God. Paul's worldly eyes were closed to the truth about Jesus. Now, however, he sees Christ, himself, and others through eyes enlightened by the Spirit.

Verse 17 celebrates this new life as a new creation. The old creation was cursed by human sin, but God had been at work on a new creation. The final touches of the new heavens and new earth await the Lord's return, but Christians have already become part of the new creation. The old things of a life of sin have passed, away and everything has become new.

Paul was writing here of the radical change that takes place when a sinner turns to Christ and passes from death to life. Other passages show that the new creation is not yet perfect. We still live in the old world and are tempted toward the old ways. A struggle between flesh and Spirit continues, although the ultimate outcome is assured for those who have truly become new in Christ (Gal. 5:13–26).

2. Reconciled and reconciling (5:18–20)

18 And all things are of God, who hath reconciled us to himself by Jesus Christ, and hath given to us the ministry of reconciliation;

19 To wit, that God was in Christ, reconciling the world unto himself, not imputing their trespasses unto them; and hath committed unto us the word of reconciliation.

20 Now then we are ambassadors for Christ, as though God did beseech you by us: we pray you in Christ's stead, be ye reconciled to God.

The New Testament contains a variety of ways to describe what happens when sinners come to God through Jesus Christ. "Forgiveness" and "reconciliation" come from the area of human relations. Everyone knows about and most have experienced forgiveness and reconciliation in relations with others. The Bible describes how God forgives our sins as a barrier in order to reconcile us to Himself. All that Paul had been describing in verses 14–17 was the work of God, not of man. The same was true of reconciliation. This is what Paul meant by "all things are of God."

Verse 18 introduces the theme of reconciliation that continues through verse 20. Paul makes two main points: (1) God has reconciled us to Himself by Jesus Christ. (2) After we have been reconciled, God entrusts to us the ministry of reconciliation.

Verse 19 amplifies both points in verse 18, especially the first one. How did God go about reconciling us to Himself by Jesus Christ? Three things stand out:

1. This was the work of God. The Bible never speaks of us reconciling God to ourselves. He is always the One who does the reconciling. In Greek religion, humans are always the ones trying to appease the gods. Humans are good and the gods are fickle, although powerful. The reverse is actually true. Humans are sinners, and God is good and gracious. He seeks to reconcile sinners to Himself. He seeks and saves the lost.

2. God did this in Christ. The words "in Christ" can refer to God at work during the incarnate ministry and death of Christ. In other words, the death of Christ does not just reveal the love of Jesus but also the love of God (Rom. 5:6–8). Or the words "in Christ" can refer to the work of God in the human experience by the power and presence of the Spirit of the crucified and risen Lord.

3. Forgiveness of sins precedes reconciliation. Sin is a barrier between sinners and God. That barrier must be removed if reconciliation is to happen. Through the death of Christ, God paid the price for our sins. When sinners repent of sin and turn in faith to Christ, God no longer counts our trespasses against us. This leads to reconciliation with God.

Verse 20 amplifies the last parts of verses 18 and 19 concerning our ministry of reconciliation. The word *ambassadors* was used in Paul's day to refer to a personal legate or representative of the emperor. This was the title of the official appointed by the emperor to rule in his stead over provinces under direct imperial control. Other provinces were called senatorial provinces. However, the title was also used for the emperor's envoy or ambassador who was sent to make peace with groups that had been at war or in rebellion against Rome. The ambassador's role was to bring them into the family of Rome.

Thus, Christians are personal representatives of Christ who go forth into a world that is in rebellion against God. Their task is to announce the good news that God offers forgiveness of all that was done during the period of rebellion and to welcome them into the family of God. Even though they have been enemies, God offers to accept them as friends and even as adopted children in full reconciliation with Him. Thus, the ambassadors are there in Christ's stead to beseech sinners, "Be ye reconciled to God."

3. Good news for sinners (5:21)

> **21 For he hath made him to be sin for us, who knew no sin; that we might be made the righteousness of God in him.**

This verse makes three points:

1. Jesus lived a sinless life. This is the consistent testimony of the New Testament. His disciples, who spent several years with Him, testified to it. Jesus had no consciousness of personal sin. Even His enemies had to come up with false charges against Him.

2. God "made him to be sin for us." This probes the deepest mystery of the Cross. Jesus, who had no sin, died a sinner's death for those who are sinners. The agony He endured was not just the agony of crucifixion but also the agony of bearing the sins of the world.

3. Jesus' death enables us to "be made the righteousness of God in him." This focuses on justification, the process of declaring sinners right with God on the basis of Christ's death (Rom. 3:20–26). Although we are guilty sinners, God acquits us of our sins and declares us right with God (Rom. 4:5). Justification leads to sanctification—the process by which God's Spirit produces in believers a new kind of righteousness (Rom. 8:1–11).

SUMMARY OF BIBLE TRUTHS

1. Awareness of our accountability to God motivates us to be sincere and unselfish.
2. Concern for others motivates Christian service.
3. Christ's sacrificial love for us motivates us to live not for ourselves but for Him.
4. Christians are new creations who see everything differently.
5. God in Christ seeks to reconcile sinners to Himself, and then entrusts the ministry of reconciliation to them.
6. The sinless Christ bore our sins so that we might be declared righteous by God.

APPLYING THE BIBLE

1. A satisfied customer. There was once a seventeen-year-old boy who was in trouble. A friend from school asked a Christian youth leader to share Christ with the boy. On a Thursday night, after an hour's discussion of the gospel, the boy received Christ. That was the first time in his life he had heard the gospel. Later that boy married his concerned schoolmate and became a pastor. The couple have a son in the pastoral ministry and two daughters who married pastors. The other daughter led a university student to Christ, married him later, and they are now very active servants of Christ in a local New Testament church. That former seventeen-year-old is now writing these lines! Don't think of me as a minister; think of me as a satisfied customer!

2. Winning others to Jesus. Comment on the implications of the following for evangelism:

▶ When the Lord came to you, He was attempting to get through you to somebody else.

▶ "We cannot but speak the things which we have seen and heard" (Acts 4:20). (Did you ever attempt to introduce somebody you had never met?)

▶ "Silver and gold have I none; but such as I have give I thee" (Acts 3:6).

▶ A formerly blind man whom Jesus had healed "answered and said, Whether he (Jesus) be a sinner or no, I know not: one thing I know, that, whereas I was blind, now I see" (John 9:25).

▶ "Go home to thy friends, and tell them how great things the Lord hath done for thee, and hath had compassion on thee" (Mark 5:19). Note the word *friends*, and that what Jesus did for him was interpreted as an act of "compassion." How is evangelism an act of compassion? Is there any greater act of compassion than leading a person to Christ?)

3. We are God's agents of reconciliation. Revelation 22:17 says, "And the Spirit (the Holy Spirit) and the bride (the church) say, Come. And let him that heareth (the evangelized) say, Come (and thus, become the evangelizer!). And let him that is athirst (him who is under conviction by the Holy Spirit) come. And whosoever will (whoever has a desire to), let him take the water of life freely." The reconciled becomes the agent of reconciliation, as Paul says in today's focal passage. Every evangelist of whatever sort was once a mission field! That makes a lot of sense. Who else could better understand? Or understand at all! Even the angels would be totally unequipped for the task, as Peter says in 1 Peter 1:12. Think about this and make a list of the angels' privileges, but you can never say they were ever redeemed by Christ!

4. Reconciliation is a possibility. Of critical importance: The message of the gospel is not "Rejoice, you have been reconciled," but, "Repent and be (that is, become) reconciled." All authentic New Testament evangelism operates on the presupposition that people are not naturally, or automatically, reconciled to God. Nobody will ever become reconciled to God apart from God's act and our appropriate life-changing response to His act. The good news is not a palliative; it is a possibility. It is not initially an invitation to rest; it is an imperative to respond. Henry David Thoreau (of Walden Pond fame) was once asked if he was at peace with God. His answer was, "I was not aware we had quarrelled." But we have! If man and God were not "at odds" (at "enmity," to use Paul's expression in Romans 8:7), Paul's use of the word *reconcile* in our focal passage would be meaningless.

5. Faithful witness? We will answer to God as to how faithfully we have called others to be reconciled to Christ. If it is true, as has commonly been reported for years, that 95 percent of all Christians have never shared their faith, we desperately need to take Paul's word to heart. Discuss these questions: What is it that prevents most Christians from sharing their faith? Are those perspectives legitimate? What can be done to alleviate those hindrances? What is your church doing to encourage members to be more faithful witnesses?

TEACHING THE BIBLE

▶ *Main Idea:* Reconciling the world to Christ is the job of every believer.
▶ *Suggested Teaching Aim:* To lead adults to identify ways they can be ambassadors for Christ.

A TEACHING OUTLINE

Reconciling the World to Christ

1. *Motives for Ministry (2 Cor. 5:11–15)*
2. *Ministry of Reconciliation (2 Cor. 5:16–21)*

Introduce the Bible Study

Point out that this lesson continues the survey of the New Testament by looking at one of the New Testament's most important doctrines—reconciliation. Share "A satisfied customer" in "Applying the Bible." Suggest that today's lesson will help members identify ways they can be ambassadors for Christ.

Search for Biblical Truth

IN ADVANCE, copy the four summary statements in "Outline and Summary" on one color of paper and the Scripture references on another color. Place both of these at random around the room. Ask members to search the Scripture and to match the statement with the appropriate Scripture.

On a chalkboard or a large sheet of paper, write: "1. Motives for Ministry (2 Cor. 5:11–15)." Ask members to look at these five verses and find three motives for ministry (v. 11—personal accountability, vv. 12–13—concern for others, vv. 14–15—love for Christ.) Lecture briefly to explain (1) what Paul meant by "knowing the terror of the Lord" (He feared not to preach because he knew God held him and all believers accountable for sharing the Word); (2) the meaning of "beside ourselves" and "sober" (v. 13); the word "constraineth" (v. 14). Ask: According to verse 15, what negative aspect does Christ's death provide? (Not live unto themselves.) Positive? (Live for Christ.)

On a chalkboard or a large sheet of paper, write: "2. Ministry of Reconciliation (2 Cor. 5:16–21)." Ask members to read these verses silently. Read verse 16 in a modern translation. Ask: What did looking at Jesus through worldly eyes cause Paul to do? (Persecute Jesus' followers.) What are some things that become new when a person is reconciled to Christ?

Ask: What two aspects of reconciliation does Paul state in verse 18? (God has reconciled us to Himself by Jesus; after we have been reconciled, God entrusts to us the ministry of reconciliation.) Lecture briefly, covering these three points about how God reconciled us to Himself by Jesus: (1) This was God's work; (2) God did this in Christ; (3) forgiveness of sins precedes reconciliation. Explain the role of an "ambassador" in Paul's day.

Ask, What does verse 21 tell us about Jesus? (Your members may suggest different ideas but consider these suggestions: Jesus lived a sinless life, God treated Him as a sinner, His death enables Jesus to make us acceptable to God.)

Prepare a brief lecture to summarize this lesson by reading and explaining each of the six statements in "Summary of Bible Truths."

Give the Truth a Personal Focus

Ask, How can you be an ambassador for Christ this coming week? How were you an ambassador this past week? Point out that reconciling the world to Christ is the job of every believer.

Confident Hope

Background Passages: Titus 2:11–14; Hebrews 12:18–29;
Revelation 1:14–20; 11:15–19
Focal Passages: Titus 2:11–14; Hebrews 12:26–29; Revelation
1:17–20; 11:15

New Testament Christians had a confident hope that was rooted in
Jesus Christ and impacted their daily living. Three passages from the last
period of New Testament history illustrate such hope. Titus 2:11–14
shows how hope relates to other aspects of salvation and how all these
transform daily living. Hebrews 12:26–29 focuses on God's unshakable
kingdom. Passages from Revelation highlight Christ's incarnate victory
and His ultimate victory.

▶**Study Aim:** *To testify of the basis of their confident hope and
of the differences it makes in how they live.*

STUDYING THE BIBLE

OUTLINE AND SUMMARY
  I.   **Salvation: Past, Present, and Future (Titus 2:11–14)**
       1. **Salvation that transforms (2:11–12)**
       2. **Liberated from sin unto good works (2:13–14)**
 II.   **Unshakable Kingdom (Heb. 12:18–29)**
       1. **Mount Sinai and Mount Zion (12:18–24)**
       2. **Exhortation and warning (12:25–29)**
III.   **Victory of Christ (Rev. 1:13–20; 11:15–19)**
       1. **Victorious Lord among His churches
          (Rev. 1:14–20)**
       2. **Proclamation of final victory (11:15–19)**

Salvation not only means forgiveness but also results in transformed
lives (Titus 2:11–12). The Lord liberates us from sin and for good works
(Titus 2:13–14). The new covenant has blessings unknown under the old
covenant (Heb. 12:18–24). Christians can worship and serve God with
the security that God's kingdom alone is eternal (Heb. 12:25–29). The
Lord who conquered death is with His people (Rev. 1:14–20). God and
Christ will ultimately be recognized as sovereign over all things (Rev.
11:15–19).

I. Salvation: Past, Present, and Future (Titus 2:11–14)
1. Salvation that transforms (2:11–12)

   11 For the grace of God that bringeth salvation hath
   appeared to all men,

   12 Teaching us that, denying ungodliness and worldly lusts,
   we should live soberly, righteously, and godly, in this present
   world.

Titus, along with the two letters to Timothy, constitute Paul's Pastoral
Letters and were written late in his life. The letter to Titus concentrates

on sound doctrine and godly living. Paul insisted that these two essentials were inseparable. Titus 2:11–14 makes two strong points: (1) God's salvation in Christ includes what He did in Christ and what He will do when Christ returns, and (2) this salvation motivates and empowers godly living.

The themes of salvation by grace for all people are familiar themes in Paul's writings. The word *appeared* shows that Paul was thinking not only of our personal experience of salvation but of God's saving work in Jesus Christ's first appearing.

God's purpose in salvation went beyond forgiveness. It also led to a new way of living. Paul used the word *teaching* to describe the impact of salvation on daily living. The word includes both instruction and discipline. Its impact leads us to renounce sinful living and to embrace godly living.

2. Liberated from sin unto good works (2:13–14)

13 Looking for that blessed hope, and the glorious appearing of the great God and our Saviour Jesus Christ;

14 Who gave himself for us, that he might redeem us from all iniquity, and purify unto himself a peculiar people, zealous of good works.

The noun translated "appearing" is from the verb "appeared" in verse 11. The noun is sometimes used by Paul of Christ's incarnate appearing (2 Tim. 1:10), but more often of His future appearing as it is in verse 13 (1 Tim. 6:14; 2 Tim. 4:1, 8). His victory over sin and death guarantees His final victory over these enemies.

This coming Savior is the same Redeemer who gave Himself to redeem us. The word *redeem* came from the slave market, where slaves could be set free by paying the redemption price. This liberation includes not only being set free from all iniquity but also being set free to be God's special people, zealous for good works.

"Looking for" denotes the earnest expectation that is part of Christian hope. The other two elements in Christian hope are desire and confidence. This blessed and glorious hope means the coming of none other that the divine Savior Jesus Christ.

Paul elsewhere clearly denied that good works are the root of our salvation (see, for example, Titus 3:4–5), but he was equally emphatic to insist that "good works" are the fruit of our salvation (Eph. 2:8–10; Gal. 5:13–26).

II. Unshakable Kingdom (Heb. 12:18–29)
1. Mount Sinai and Mount Zion (12:18–24)

The theme of the book of Hebrews is the superiority of the new covenant to the old covenant. Hebrews 12:18–24 contrasts the two covenants by contrasting Israel's experiences at Mount Sinai with Christians' past, present, and future experiences at Mount Zion—the blessings of the new covenant to culminate in the heavenly Jerusalem. Reading Exodus 19:10–25; 20:18–21 shows that the writer did not exaggerate the Israelites' fear at Mount Sinai, which is highlighted in Hebrews 12:18–21.

Hebrews 12:22–24 emphasizes that believers have already entered into the foretaste of the full joys of the future heavenly city.

2. Exhortation and warning (12:25–29)

26 Whose voice then shook the earth: but now he hath promised, saying, Yet once more I shake not the earth only, but also heaven.

27 And this word, Yet once more, signifieth the removing of those things that are shaken, as of things that are made, that those things which cannot be shaken may remain.

28 Wherefore we receiving a kingdom which cannot be moved, let us have grace, whereby we may serve God acceptably with reverence and godly fear:

29 For our God is a consuming fire.

The book of Hebrews is a book of doctrinal truths with interspersed exhortations (13:22). The exhortations combine warnings with challenges. Hebrews 12:25 is typical of a familiar theme of the exhortations: to hear and heed the voice of the Lord Jesus (see 2:1–4). The contrasts between Mount Sinai and Mount Zion were not intended to point up a God of wrath against a God of love. The Old Testament shows God's mercy, and the New Testament presents God's judgment against sin. For example, Hebrews 12:23 describes the God of the new covenant as "the Judge of all." Hebrews 12:29 warns that "our God is a consuming fire" (compare Heb. 10:31).

God shook the ground at Mount Sinai (12:26a; Exod. 19:18). He will shake all things in the final days. This final shaking mentioned in 12:26b is a quotation from Haggai 2:6–7. This shaking will mark the end of all things earthly and transient so "that those things which cannot be shaken may remain." The eternal kingdom of God alone will withstand the final shaking. Earthly nations, institutions, and possessions will perish; but God and His kingdom will endure. Verse 27 calls Christians to express gratitude ("grace") to God for an unshakable kingdom. Such gratitude ought to motivate us to "serve God with reverence and godly fear" as we await the fulfillment of this confident hope.

III. Victory of Christ (Rev. 1:13–20; 11:15–19)

1. Victorious Lord among His churches (1:14–20)

17 And when I saw him, I fell at his feet as dead. And he laid his right hand upon me, saying unto me, Fear not; I am the first and the last:

18 I am he that liveth, and was dead; and, behold, I am alive for evermore, Amen; and have the keys of hell and of death.

19 Write the things which thou hast seen, and the things which are, and the things which shall be hereafter;

20 The mystery of the seven stars which thou sawest in my right hand, and the seven golden candlesticks. The seven stars are the angels of the seven churches: and the seven candlesticks which thou sawest are the seven churches.

Revelation was written to Christians who were being persecuted (1:9). This was probably the persecution conducted by the emperor Domitian toward the end of the first century. The persecuted Christians were wondering: "Where is the Lord? Will He be victorious?" The vision of a glorified Son of man and His words in Revelation 1:14–20 answered the first question. The vision is in verses 14–16. John and his readers had little doubt that John saw a vision of the exalted Lord Jesus. The name and description fit Him alone.

As was often the response to heavenly visions, John fell at His feet like a dead man. As was usually the response of the Lord, He said, "Fear not." In Isaiah 44:6, God said, "I am the first, and I am the last." The divine Lord used the same title in verse 17.

Verse 18 proclaims the Lord's incarnate victory over death. He is the living One; He died; but now He is alive forever. The word translated "hell" is *hades*, the Greek word for the place of the dead. In the New Testament it usually refers to the place of the departed dead (Acts 2:27), but sometimes to the place of the wicked dead (Luke 16:23). This is not the word *gehenna*, the place of eternal punishment (Matt. 5:22; 18:9). Revelation 6:8 describes a vision of death as riding on a pale horse and followed by "Death and Hades." The point in Revelation 1:18 is that because of His victory over sin and death, the Lord Jesus has the keys to death and the grave (see 1 Cor. 15:55–57).

Some Bible students see verse 19 as an outline of the book. "The things which thou hast seen" is the vision of chapter 1. "The things which are" are the visions of Revelation 2–3. "The things which shall be" are visions of the future in the rest of the book. Other Bible students see the book as rooted in a first-century persecution ("the things which are") with visions of past, present, and future growing out of the key vision of Revelation 1:14–20. The victorious Lord speaks encouragement to believers of every generation. He bases it on His already accomplished victory at the cross and the empty tomb. He extends it to assure us of His final victory over sin, death, and Satan.

Verse 20 refers back to seven lampstands ("candlesticks") and seven stars. He was standing among the lampstands (1:13). He held the stars in His hand (1:16). The stars are either human or divine guardians of the churches. The lampstands are the churches. Thus, the picture is of the living, victorious Lord standing among His churches with their guardians securely in His hand. This was the Lord's answer to "Where is the Lord?" His answer was, "I am right here with you and among you."

2. Proclamation of final victory (11:15–19)

> **15 And the seventh angel sounded; and there were great voices in heaven, saying, The kingdoms of this world are become the kingdoms of our Lord, and of His Christ; and he shall reign for ever and ever.**

The book of Revelation does wait until the final chapter to announce the outcome of the story. At several places in the book, the readers are assured of the ultimate triumph of God and His Son. Verse 15 is such a verse. The end is proclaimed, although it is not described until later. The word translated "kingdoms" is actually singular, meaning "kingdom" or "reign." In other words, during human history only people of faith recognize God's sovereign rule over all things; most people assume that earthly governments and rulers reign. Verse 15 announces the time when all human sovereignty will end and God and Christ will be recognized by all as holding the only sovereign power (see Ps. 2; Dan. 2:44; Phil. 2:9–11; 1 Cor. 15:24–28).

At this announcement, the redeemed (twenty-four elders) praise the Lord who will reign forever (11:16–17). This will mean judgment for those who have rebelled against the divine sovereignty (11:18–19).

SUMMARY OF BIBLE TRUTHS

1. Salvation is rooted in the past, is being experienced in the present, and will be consummated in the future.
2. Salvation results in transformed lives.
3. God's judgment will destroy all earthly things.
4. Christians rejoice because God's kingdom is unshakable.
5. Christ, who conquered death, is with His people during times of trouble.
6. God and Christ will finally be acknowledged as having the only sovereign rule.

APPLYING THE BIBLE

1. Jesus Christ—the only hope. Alexander Pope wrote, "Hope springs eternal in the human heart." Powerful as that sentiment is, it is not true. The world is full of hopeless people, as every observer of humanity knows. That hopelessness derives, essentially, from the fact that they do not live in the "unshakable kingdom," which the writer of Hebrews—and all other Christians—know about.

2. We need hope. D. Elton Trueblood wrote, "It has been said that man is the only animal who laughs, and the only one who weeps; the only one who prays; the only one who walks fully erect; the only one who makes fires; the only one who guides his own destiny; the only one who is penitent; and the only one who needs to be." It could also be said, truthfully and intriguingly, that man is the only animal who hopes! Or needs to![1]

3. There is more beyond here. "Before Columbus set sail to cross the Atlantic, it was believed that the world ended out there somewhere past Gibraltar. To the Spanish, one of their real glories was that they were the last outpost of the world, and that their country fronted right on the great beyond. Spain's royal coat of arms showed the Pillars of Hercules, the great columns guarding the Strait of Gibraltar, and the royal motto said plainly *Ne Plus Ultra*, meaning, roughly, 'There is no more beyond here.' But then, when Columbus returned, he had actually discovered a whole new world out there. The ancient motto was now meaningless. In this crisis someone at Court made a noble and thrifty suggestion, which was immediately adopted by Queen Isabella. It was simply that the first word, Ne, be deleted. Now the motto or the coat of arms read—and has read ever since—just two words: Plus Ultra—'There is plenty more beyond.'" What a perfect description of the$_2$Christian's hope! Plus Ultra! Let's change it and make Plus Ultra Ultra!^{2}

4. Are your hopes too small? "Reaching beyond their wildest imagination, [the city fathers of New York City] drew streets on the map all the way out to 19th Street. They called it 'Boundary Street' because they were sure that was as large as the city would ever become. But history has proven them to be shortsighted. At last count, the city had reached 284th Street—far beyond their expectations."

5. Hope or suicide. Charles Colson writes of the hopelessness of Ernest Hemingway (and his existentialist friends): "As Hemingway's frind Jean-Paul Sartre put it, 'On a shattered and deserted stage, without script, director, prompter, or audience, the actor is free to improvise his own part.' This view sounds both reasonable and romantic in literature or discussions in cafes and coffee bars. But the prospect in real life is stark. Among those who 'tie a lamp to the masthead and steer by that' when 'the stars are quenched in heaven,' few take their existential belief to the ultimate conclusion (suicide, as with Hemingway). For this comfortless doctrine shreds the very fibers and design of the human$_3$psyche. We need more. And most of us—deep down—cannot deny it."^{3}

6. A positive approach. Did you hear about the hopeful boy who came home with bad grades on his arithmetic test? He said to his father, "Dad, I think I flunked my arithmetic test." His dad said, "Son, don't say that; that's negative. Be positive." So the boy said, "Dad, I am positive I flunked my arithmetic test!"

7. What is your hope of salvation based on? I heard about a little girl who took her birth certificate to school on her first day there—and lost it! She sat down and cried about it. The principal of the school saw her and asked what was wrong. She told him, "I've lost my paper proving I'm alive!" Ask yourself, "What is the paper proving I'm alive?"

8. Comment about these perspectives on hope:

▶ I saw a bumper sticker the other day that read: "Since I gave up hope, I feel much better."

▶ Mark Twain worked the characters in his story "The Terrible Catastrophe" into such a predicament that they couldn't get out. He concluded the story by saying, "I have these characters in such a fix I cannot get them out. Anyone who thinks he can is welcome to try!"

▶ Emil Brunner said: "What oxygen is to the lungs, hope is for man's soul."

▶ A leading politician took his life and left this note in his pocket: "I must kill myself because I cannot live without hope."

TEACHING THE BIBLE

Confident Hope
▶ *Main Idea:* Christians have a confident hope in Christ.
▶ *Suggested Teaching Aim:* To lead adults to testify of the basis of their confident hope and of the differences it makes in how they live.

A TEACHING OUTLINE

1. *Salvation: Past, Present, and Future (Titus 2:11–14)*
2. *Unshakable Kingdom (Heb. 12:18–29)*
3. *Victory of Christ (Rev. 1:13–20; 11:15–19)*

Introduce the Bible Study
Use "There is more beyond here" in "Applying the Bible" to introduce the Bible study. Say, The purpose of the lesson today is to lead adults to testify about what gives them a confident hope and how that hope makes a difference in how they live.

Search for Biblical Truth
IN ADVANCE, write the six summary statements under "Outline and Summary" on six strips of paper; write the six Scripture references on different pieces of paper. Mix up the strips and place both statements and references on the wall. Organize members in six groups and assign one of the Scripture references to each group. Ask members to search the Scripture references and find the appropriate statements.

Write on a chalkboard or a large sheet of paper, "Salvation that Transforms." Ask the group with Titus 2:11–12 to suggest their statement. Say: The Book of Titus, along with 1, 2 Timothy make up Paul's Pastoral Letters. Titus concentrates on two essentials Paul considered inseparable: sound doctrine and godly living. Ask members to identify these two essentials in these verses. (v. 11—doctrine of God's salvation; v. 12—this salvation motivates and empowers godly living.)

DISCUSS: Can one be a Christian and not live like it?

Write on the chalkboard, "Liberated from Sin unto Good Works." Ask the group with Titus 2:13–14 to identify their statement. Using the material in "Studying the Bible," lecture briefly on the following words: "appearing," "redeem," "looking for," and "good works."

DISCUSS: How does Jesus' coming affect the way you live?

Write on the chalkboard, "Mount Sinai and Mount Zion." Ask the group with Hebrews 12:18–28 to identify their statement. Briefly explain the use of Mount Sinai and Mount Zion in the book of Hebrews.

Write on the chalkboard, "Exhortation and Warning." Ask the group with Hebrews 12:25–29 to identify their statement. Ask members to open their Bibles to Hebrews 12:25–29 and scan these verses. Ask: To what shaking does the writer refer in verse 26? (Ask a member to read aloud Exodus 19:18 if no one knows.) When will God shake all things? What one thing will not be shaken? How should knowing that we belong to a kingdom that cannot be shaken make us live?

DISCUSS: What part does fear play in the way you behave?

Write on the chalkboard, "Victorious Lord Among His Churches." Ask the group with Revelation 1:14–20 to identify their statement. Using the material in "Studying the Bible," lecture briefly, covering these points: (1) Christians were being persecuted by Domitian and were asking, "Where is the Lord?" (2) Christ has the keys to death and the grave;

(3) verse 19 is an outline of the book; (4) Jesus' answer to where He is, is that He is right in the midst of His churches.

DISCUSS: How does Jesus' presence affect your life each day?

Write on the chalkboard, "Proclamation of Final Victory." Ask the final group to read their statement. Ask a member to read verse 15.

DISCUSS: How does this certainty affect the way you live?

Read the six "Summary of Bible Truths" statements.

Give the Truth a Personal Focus

Write on the chalkboard, *Because of my confident hope in Christ for the past, present, and future, I . . .* Ask members to complete this statement and share with the group.

---

1. The quote is from David Elton Trueblood, cited in *The Great American Bathroom Book,* Vol. III, Compact Classics, Inc., 1994, p. 446.
2. Ibid., p. 486.
3. Charles Colson, *Kingdoms in Conflict* (Grand Rapids: Zondervan, 1987), 56.

Promote Kingdom Life

Background Passages: Matthew 18:1–10; 19:13–15
Focal Passages: Matthew 18:1–10; 19:13–15

Abortion, infanticide (killing newborns or leaving them to die or to be stolen), and abuse were common in the ancient world. The early Christians consistently opposed these evils. Their opposition was based on sharing the Old Testament view that humans are made in God's image and thus human life should be precious. They were also motivated by the words and actions of Jesus about little ones. Two such passages constitute this alternate lesson for those who want a special lesson for Sanctity of Human Life Sunday.

▶**Study Aim:** *To identify ways to adopt an active servant role in promoting the sanctity of human life.*

STUDYING THE BIBLE

OUTLINE AND SUMMARY
   I. **Kingdom Attitude (Matt. 18:1–4)**
      1. **Jesus and little children (18:1–2)**
      2. **Becoming as little children (18:3–4)**
  II. **Kingdom Acceptance (Matt. 18:5)**
 III. **Kingdom Warning (Matt. 18:6–10)**
      1. **Do not cause little ones to stumble (18:6–7)**
      2. **Do whatever it takes to avoid sin (18:8–9)**
      3. **Do not despise those whom the Father loves (18:10)**
 IV. **Kingdom Concern (Matt. 19:13–15)**
      1. **Disciples rebuked those bringing children (19:13)**
      2. **Stop hindering little children (19:14–15)**

Jesus used a little child to show who is greatest in God's kingdom (18:1–2). People enter the kingdom and achieve kingdom greatness as they become like little children (18:3–4). Welcoming little children is welcoming Jesus (18:5). Avoid causing little ones to go astray (18:6–7). Radical surgery of a body part would be better than going to hell (18:8–9). Do not despise little ones, whose angels have constant access to the Father (18:10). The disciples rebuked those who wanted to bring little children for Jesus to bless them (19:13). Encourage rather than hinder those who bring children to Jesus (19:14–15).

I. Kingdom Attitude (Matt. 18:1–4)
1. Jesus and little children (18:1–2)

> **1 At the same time came the disciples unto Jesus, saying, Who is the greatest in the kingdom of heaven?**
> **2 And Jesus called a little child unto him, and set him in the midst of them.**

Nothing shows so clearly how totally the disciples misunderstood what Jesus said about His cross and theirs (Matt. 16:22–24) as their continuing argument about which of them was the greatest (Matt. 20:17–28). On this occasion, they asked Jesus to tell them who was greatest in God's kingdom. Jesus called a little child to Him and set the child in the middle of the group of disciples.

This reveals how sensitive Jesus was to little children and how responsive they were to Him. Jesus had noticed the child nearby. Jesus practiced what He preached about loving little children (Matt. 19:13–15; Mark 9:36–37).

2. Becoming as little children (18:3–4)

3 And said, Verily I say unto you, Except ye be converted, and become as little children, ye shall not enter into the kingdom of heaven.

4 Whosoever therefore shall humble himself as this little child, the same is greatest in the kingdom of heaven.

Bible students have identified a variety of qualities of children that Jesus may have had in mind; however, two seem most likely to be models of kingdom citizens. First of all, children are dependent on adults for their care; and at least when they are small, most of them recognize that fact. In order to enter God's kingdom, people must accept their dependence on God's mercy and grace. This is why the First Beatitude is, "Blessed are the poor in spirit; for theirs is the kingdom of heaven" (Matt. 5:3). Second, children are more responsive to God's call than adults. Notice how quickly this little child came when Jesus called. Adults tend to be too aware of what people will think and say, but children recognize God's call and obey (1 Sam. 3:10; Matt. 21:15–16).

Jesus told the disciples that people needed to repent of their selfish strivings (exemplified by the disciples' argument about which of them was greatest) and become as little children. This is necessary for a person even to enter the kingdom, and the development of this quality in humble self-giving service is God's standard for measuring true greatness.

II. Kingdom Acceptance (Matt. 18:5)

5 And whoso shall receive one such little child in my name receiveth me.

The word translated "receive" means more than accepting; it usually carries the idea of welcoming. The same word was used to describe how Simeon took the infant Jesus in his arms (Luke 2:28), and how Jesus was not welcomed in Samaria (Luke 9:53) but was in Galilee (John 4:45). Mark 9:36–37, which describes this incident, says that Jesus took the child in His arms before teaching the need to receive little children.

Jesus was teaching and acting consistently with the Old Testament, which sees children as precious gifts and trusts from God (Ps. 127:3). The Law commanded that orphans be given special attention by the community along with other helpless groups like widows and resident aliens (Deut. 24:17–22; see also James 1:27).

In the Gospel accounts of the teaching about receiving little children, Jesus gave the strongest reason for Christians to welcome little children. By welcoming children, we welcome none other than Christ Himself. This is the same principle that Jesus taught in Matthew 25:34–40. When we welcome little children, we may not realize it at the time; but we are also welcoming Jesus Himself.

III. Kingdom Warning (Matt. 18:6–10)

1. Do not cause little ones to stumble (18:6–7)

6 But whoso shall offend one of these little ones which believe in me, it were better for him that a millstone were hanged about his neck, and that he were drowned in the depth of the sea.

7 Woe unto the world because of offences! for it must needs be that offences come; but woe to that man by which the offence cometh!

The word translated "offences" means something that causes someone to stumble. As applied to moral issues, it means a temptation to sin. Jesus warned against doing anything that might cause a little one to stumble or fall into sin. In verses 2–5, Jesus used the words for "child" or "children." In verses 6 and 10, he used the expression "little ones." He probably was broadening the application to include not only little children but also new converts. Jesus warned that causing either of these groups to sin is a serious sin that will receive serious punishment.

When Jesus said that "offences must needs be," He did not mean that God wants temptations or that people need them. His point is that in a sinful world, temptations are inevitable. He quickly emphasized that although temptations are inevitable, people who cause the temptations are accountable to God for leading others astray. Look at this from God's point of view. He has entrusted little children to parents and other adults. If any one of these grown-ups leads a child astray, woe to him or her!

2. Do whatever it takes to avoid sin (18:8–9)

8 Wherefore if thy hand or thy foot offend thee, cut them off, and cast them from thee: it is better for thee to enter into life halt or maimed, rather than having two hands or two feet to be cast into everlasting fire.

9 And if thine eye offend thee, pluck it out, and cast it from thee: it is better for thee to enter into life with one eye, rather than having two eyes to be cast into hell fire.

This same kind of warning is found in Matthew 5:29–30 in connection with the danger of lust for sexual immorality. Jesus was using powerful words to say that even radical surgery of a body part would be preferable to falling into sin. In other words, the focus in verses 8–9 is not on leading someone else into sin so much as allowing oneself to fall into sin. His point is to do whatever it takes to avoid sin.

Since this warning is sandwiched between warnings against leading little ones astray, Jesus may have intended it to apply to leading either ourselves or others astray. Jesus used the Greek word for hell as a place of punishment to describe how God will deal with those who lead themselves or little ones astray.

3. Do not despise those whom the Father loves (18:10)

10 Take heed that ye despise not one of these little ones; for I say unto you, That in heaven their angels do always behold the face of my Father which is in heaven.

The word *despise* literally means to "look down on." This may be expressed through everything from neglect to abuse. One expression of it is to lead others astray. Despising little ones is the opposite of welcoming them. Ancient society showed that they despised little children by practicing and condoning such things as abortion, infanticide, and child abuse.

Jesus made clear that despising little ones is to despise a group that has the Father's special love and concern. God loves everyone; but the Bible repeatedly shows that He pays special attention to weak, helpless, and mistreated groups. The last part of the verse may mean that each child has a guardian angel. It may mean that an angel represents more than one person. What is clear is that the needs of little children are constantly before the heavenly Father. He knows and cares about them.

IV. Kingdom Concern (Matt. 19:13–15)

1. Disciples rebuked those bringing children (19:13)

13 Then were there brought unto him little children, that he should put his hands on them, and pray: and the disciples rebuked them.

Matthew 19:13–15 is a case study in the principles taught in Matthew 18:1–10. It shows that the disciples had not learned the lessons Jesus was trying to teach. They rebuked those who wanted to bring little children to Jesus. The ones who brought the children were probably their parents, although the Bible does not say. Their goal was for Jesus to lay His hands on the children and pray for them. This was a common Jewish way of blessing someone.

The word *rebuked* is the same word used of Jesus' rebuke of James and John when they wanted to call down fire from heaven on the Samaritans (Luke 9:55). Imagine how the parents and the little children must have withered under the rebuke of the disciples. Why did they issue such a rebuke? Apparently, they still felt that little children were not that important to the Master. He was too busy, they reasoned, to be bothered by a group of parents and little children.

2. Stop hindering little children (19:14–15)

14 But Jesus said, Suffer little children, and forbid them not, to come unto me: for of such is the kingdom of heaven.

15 And he laid his hands on them, and departed thence.

Mark 10:14 says that Jesus was "much displeased" at what His disciples had done. He quickly told them to stop hindering these little children from coming to Him. Instead, they should not only allow but also encourage those who wanted to bring little children to come to Him.

Mark 10:16 says that Jesus took the children in His arms and blessed them. If the disciples' rebuke had withered the spirits of the parents and children, Jesus' actions caused them to bloom again with the assurance of the Father's love. Christians believe that God has revealed Himself in His Son. If we want to know what God is like, we read the Gospels and note what Jesus said and did. In Matthew 18:10, Jesus said that the Father loves little children. In Matthew 19:14–15, Jesus revealed that love by His actions.

SUMMARY OF BIBLE TRUTHS

1. Jesus revealed God's love for children by His teachings and actions.
2. Be as dependent on and as responsive to God as little children are.
3. Welcome little children, for in so doing you welcome Jesus.
4. Do not lead astray or hurt little ones.
5. Do not despise little ones by neglect or by abuse.
6. Encourage rather than discourage little children and those who bring them to Jesus.

APPLYING THE BIBLE

1. The original Hippocratic oath. In the famed Hippocratic oath, dating back to four hundred years before Christ, those pursuing medicine were required to swear, "I will give no deadly medicine to anyone if asked, nor suggest any such counsel; furthermore, I will not give to a woman an instrument to produce abortion."

2. The first generation. In his novel *The Thanatos Syndrome,* Walker Percy describes an exchange between an old priest and a psychiatrist in which the old priest says, "You are a member of the first generation of doctors in the history of medicine to turn their backs on the oath of Hippocrates and kill millions of old, useless people, unborn children, born malformed children."[1]

3. Infanticide is nothing new. During New Testament times, a Roman named Hilarion wrote a letter to his wife Alis containing the following message: "Know that we are still in Alexandria. Do not be anxious; if they really go home, I will remain in Alexandria. I beg and entreat you, take care of the little one, and as soon as we receive our pay, I will send it up to you. If by chance you bear a child, if it is a boy, let it be, if it is a girl, cast it out."[2]

4. Femicide—for girls only. Charles Colson refers to the practice of "female feticide," which is taking the lives of female fetuses and not of male ones. (Some call it "femicide.") "One study revealed that out of 8,000 Bombay abortions, 7,999 involved a female fetus." Ask yourself these questions: Is it worse to take the life of a fetus because of its sex? Is it rational to argue that a woman has the complete right to abort a fetus and yet wrong to abort on the basis of sexual preference? Is the growing practice of "abortion reduction," that is, the aborting of one or more fetuses where there is a multiple pregnancy, ethical?

5. Christians have opposed abortion for many centuries. What did the early Christians believe about abortion? The *Didache*, doctrinal compendium dated from about A.D. 140, instructed Christians: "You shall not kill the fetus by abortion nor destroy the infant already born." The Letter to Diognetus, an anonymous second-century letter, says, "(To the Christians) every foreign land is . . . as their native country. . . . They marry . . . they beget children; but they do not destroy their offspring. They have a common table, but not a common bed." Tertullian (A.D. 160–230) wrote in his *Apology,* "To hinder a birth is merely a speedier man-killing; nor does it matter whether you take away a life that is born, or destroy one that is coming to the birth."

6. An expert speaks. I am writing these lines on the morning after our annual crisis pregnancy center banquet. We heard the famed medical doctor, John C. Willke. He has been involved in the abortion issue on the national and international scene since 1971, two years before *Roe v Wade.* Dr. Willke said that he and his wife have settled on several actions that they strongly suggest be followed. In the experience of many counselors, the last one is the most difficult to achieve. (1) What are you and the members of your church doing to minister to such people? (2) How do you deal with church members who might be afraid to minister to them? Or who don't think they "deserve" it, etc.? (3) Are the five suggested actions mentioned earlier biblical? (4) What other biblical insights are available for those who have experienced abortions:

▶ Stop suppressing it; tell a few trusted "significant others."
▶ Grieve; not to do so, as always in traumatic situations, prevents healing.
▶ Seek and accept God's forgiveness.
▶ Forgive others—the one who fathered the child, those who counseled abortion, organizations that have made it sound easy and uncomplicated (and right!).
▶ Forgive yourself. Many counselors find that this is the most difficult step of all.

7. Wait a minute! A college class had this problem put to them by a professor: "A certain man has syphilis; his wife has tuberculosis; of their four children, one has died, and the other three suffer from an incurable illness that is considered terminal. The mother is pregnant. What do you recommend?" Abortion was recommended by the majority of the students. "Fine," countered the professor. "You have just killed Beethoven!"

TEACHING THE BIBLE

▶ *Main Idea:* God's people should respect all forms of human life.
▶ *Suggested Teaching Aim:* To identify ways to adopt an active servant role in promoting the sanctity of human life.

A TEACHING OUTLINE

Promote Kingdom Life

1. *Kingdom Attitude (Matt. 18: 1–4)*
2. *Kingdom Acceptance (Matt. 18:5)*
3. *Kingdom Warning (Matt. 18:6–10)*
4. *Kingdom Concern (Matt. 19:13–15)*

Introduce the Bible Study

Ask: What would you give in exchange for your life? What would you give in exchange for someone else's life? Point out that all life is precious—unborn or living.

Search for Biblical Truth

IN ADVANCE, make a teaching outline poster by copying the four points on strips of paper. Place the first point on the focal wall. **IN ADVANCE,** enlist a reader to read the Scripture when you call for it. Ask for Matthew 18:1–4 to be read at this time. Ask, What prompted the disciples' question? (Their concern for power.) What qualities of children make them models of kingdom citizens? (Dependent on adults for their care and responsive to God's call.) How do these two qualities relate to entering the kingdom of God?

Place the second outline point on the wall. Ask the reader to read verse 5. If members have different translations, ask them to read the verse in their translations.

DISCUSS: If people welcome Jesus when they welcome a child, what do they do when they abuse a child?

Place the third outline point on the wall. Ask the reader to read verses 6–7.

DISCUSS: How can adults offend children? (List these ways on a chalkboard.)

Ask the reader to read verses 8–9.

DISCUSS: Based upon the list compiled above, how seriously should we take this admonition for radical surgery?

Ask the reader to read verse 10. Using the material in "Studying the Bible," explain the reference to angels.

Place the fourth outline point on the wall. Ask the reader to read Matthew 19:13. Explain the practice of asking a famous rabbi to bless their children. Ask, What does this verse show about how much the disciples learned from Jesus' earlier lesson? Why do you think the disciples rebuked those bringing the children to Jesus?

Ask the reader to read verses 14–15. Ask: If Jesus was concerned for children, how concerned should we be? Do churches abuse children when they fail to provide adequate facilities for them?

DISCUSS: How do you think Jesus will respond to a church that fails to set up adequate standards for its children's workers to make sure that workers do not sexually abuse children in their care?

IN ADVANCE, write the six statements in "Summary of Bible Truths" on six small strips. Enlist two members to read the statements alternately to summarize the lesson.

Give the Truth a Personal Focus

Organize members into groups of two or three. On a chalkboard write: *Since promoting the welfare of children is a task close to the heart of Jesus, what can we do to promote their welfare?* Ask the small groups to discuss this question for two minutes, then call for reports

---

1. Quoted in Charles Colson, *The God of Stones and Spiders* (Wheaton: Crossway, 1990), 48.
2. Quoted from C. K. Barrett, ed., *New Testament Documents: Selected Documents* (San Francisco: Harper, 1987).